Vedic Astrology

A Journey Through History, Principles And Mathematical Foundations

Srinivasan Gopalan

Publisher
UNICORN BOOKS
F-2/16, Ansari Road, Daryaganj, New Delhi-110002
☎ 011-23262683, 23250704
E-mail: info@unicornbooks.in • *Website:* www.unicornbooks.in

ISBN 978-81-7806-362-1

Vedic Astrology (English)

Edition: 2026

Printed at : Param Offsetters, Okhla, New Delhi-110020.

This book is humbly
dedicated to
my grandfather
Dr. N.P.Seshadri

Preface

The ancient science of Vedic astrology has been talked about and practiced since time immemorial. Practitioners and researchers of this widely debated science would attest to the fact that Vedic astrology as a topic is vast as an ocean and takes several years if not a lifetime to comprehend, analyse and prognosticate the occurrence of a future event or phenomena. Its concepts are however very simple; its tools and techniques are based on the fundamental power of counting (computing) and its principles are as logical as they can be. Astrology has not only been a subject of adulation but also one of scorn and derision. Disbelievers classify Vedic astrology as being a pseudoscience useful only for the gullible. An often asked question is "How can celestial objects such as planets control us"? They are right. Planets do not control human beings. It is there relative positioning on a time scale that seems to affect the decisions that we humans make which ultimately determine the various events that occur in our lives. Think about an extremely hot summer day. At 6AM on a Sunday morning we perhaps could see several people in a park for a morning jog or walk. Would we see as many people at 3PM on the same day? Similarly, on a bitterly cold winter Sunday, we might not see anyone taking a brisk morning walk at 6AM but might see some persons doing the same around mid-day. The only difference in the above instances is the change in time and season as a result of the movement of the Sun in the sky. This is a classic case of planetary motion affecting human behaviour. In fact the beauty in the study of Vedic astrology lies in its application more than its principles. A rasi chart is used by many practitioners in providing forecasts about an individual. If the forecast turns out to be reasonably accurate, both the astrologer and astrology are held in awe by the individual, else both are subject to much criticism. In reality the rasi chart is the primary chart that should be used in making forecasts but can only provide a directional pointer on potential outcomes based on the decisions the individual has made or plans to take. This must be supported by the divisional charts of astrology, as otherwise the forecasts could turn out to be completely inaccurate. Each of these divisional charts signifies a particular aspect of the individual. Vedic Astrology is very unique in that it introduces the concept of Dasa and Bhukti something not used in western astrology. Its principles which have been derived based on numerous observations and empirical computations are easy to absorb. For example, the Earth's only satellite Moon which is a planet in Vedic astrology is considered to be the significator of the human mind, quite simply because it is the closest celestial body from the Earth. Vedic Astrology has also given us the 7 days of the week derived from the concept of Hora used in determining the quality of time. The Hindu calendar or the panchangam has been used for several centuries describing and forecasting natural as well as celestial occurrences. It computes and describes among other numerical data the position of Sun, Moon and other planets including the nodes of the Moon, the concept of the phases of the Moon which we learn in our Physics lectures, constellations planets traverse through as well as the occurrences of celestial phenomena such as the eclipses. In fact a rasi chart can be used to predict the next occurrence of a potential eclipse for any given year. Vedic timekeeping introduced the smallest and largest measures of time while the 12 zodiac signs popular among the masses are said to be nothing but the limbs of the supreme Lord Maha Vishnu. Forecasting the outcome of events in an individual's life can be a complicated task but the planetary positions at the time of birth as well as the rising sign or Lagna can definitely indicate the course of action an individual might undertake when faced with a particular situation. This book illustrates with numerical examples the basic concepts of Vedic astrology coupled with astronomical principles that are applied rigorously by the practitioners of this ancient science. It is also laced with some popular historical facts. I hope you will enjoy your journey of this book.

Acknowledgement

A book is rarely an individual effort as many minds are involved in its publication. I would like to thank Unicorn Books and Dr. Ashok Gupta for giving me this opportunity to bring out this book on Vedic astrology. I would also like to thank my family members especially my mother Raji Gopalan, my father R. Gopalan and my sister Swetha for being a constant source of support and encouragement. And finally to you the reader, this book would not be what it is without your interest and support. I hope this book goes a considerable way in enriching your knowledge on Vedic astrology.

Contents

1. History of Vedic Astrology 9
2. Tropical and Sidereal Astrology (Western Vs. Vedic) 14
3. 12 Zodiacs or Rasis 21
4. Panchangam and Timekeeping 39
5. Nakshatras 49
6. Tithis 66
7. Yogas 73
8. Karanas 80
9. Sun Signs 83
10. Moon Signs 84
11. The 9 Planets (Navagrahas) of Vedic Astrology 86
12. Planetary Terminologies 96
13. Ascendant / Lagna 105
14. 12 Houses of A Rasi/Birth Chart (How to Construct Your Birth Chart / Horoscope) 120
15. Dasa + Bhukti / Main-Period + Sub-Period 143
16. Gochara Transit 153

Appendix

1. Rasimana + Charakhanda 159
2. Equation of Time 162

3. Sidereal Time 165
4. Longitude of Sun and Moon 167
5. Auspicious and Inauspicious Times 171
6. Table of Navagrahas 175

1

History of Vedic Astrology

The ancient science of Vedic astrology could be traced back to the vedas to around 5000 BCE. The vedas are books of knowledge that hold a position of unique reverence in Hinduism and are among the world's most ancient and sacred texts.

The four sacred books of the vedas are:-

- Rigveda
- Yajurveda
- Samaveda
- Atharvaveda

Each of the vedas consists of four parts, namely, Mantra-Samhitas or hymns, Brahmanas or explanations of mantras or rituals, Aranyakas or philosophical interpretations of the rituals, Upanishads or the art of self-realization. Furthermore, the division of each veda into four parts relates to the four stages of human life, namely, Brahmacharya or student (1st quarter), Grihastha or householder (2nd quarter), Vanaprastha or retirement (3rd quarter), and Sanyasa or ascetic (last quarter).

Each of the vedas consists of a subsidiary which is referred to as the Upvedas.

Arthveda is a subsidiary of the Rigveda, and relates to the science of sociology and economics.

Dhanurveda is a subsidiary of the Yajurveda, and relates to military science, including the martial arts.

Gandharvaveda is a subsidiary of the Samaveda, and relates to the arts and music.

Ayurveda is a subsidiary of the Atharvaveda, and relates to medical science.

According to some Vedic astrologers one of the first references to astrology dates back to the Rig Veda, the oldest of the 4 texts which records a description of the chakra or wheel of 360°. The Vedas were divided into the vedangas (ved meaning knowledge and angas meaning limbs). These texts embodied the ved purush or cosmic individual and also enable us to realize our supreme soul. There are six vedangas or parts of the vedas:-

Jyotish: The study of astronomy and astrology

Kalpa: The study of sacred rites and rituals

Nirukta: The study of etymology

Shiksha:The study of phonetics Vyakarana: The study of grammar

Chanda: The study of the structure of poetry

Each of the vedangas is associated with a body part that comprises the ved purush. Jyotish represents the eyes of ved purush and is an important key to help us realize our true soul nature. Jyotish is the study of the light of celestial bodies. It consists of the study of astronomy which is the science of the movements of the celestial bodies and astrology which delves into the study of the influence of the celestial bodies on our lives. Jyotish shastra or the science of vedic astrology, is a compilation of 4,00,000 verses and consists of 3 main branches.

Siddhanta or Ganita deals with the mathematical calculations, the methodology of calculating planetary positions, knowledge about time, place, direction, eclipses, their rising and setting, planetary movements, conjunctions, aspects, retrogression etc.

Jataka or Hora deals with the techniques of interpretation of horoscopes of individuals. It describes signs, planets, their qualities, circumstances at the time of birth, arishta (mishaps), longevity of the native, different dasa systems and their results, profession (sources of livelihood), ashtakavarga, varied types of yogas, results of planetary positions in different houses, signs, nakshatras, aspects of planets, planetary combinations, female horoscopy, circumstances at the time of death, cases of unknown birth time etc. This branch also deals with selecting a Muhurtha or auspicious time for an activity.

Samhita deals with all that is related to the masses and is a compilation of varied subjects like the results of rising and setting of planets, appearance of different types of comets, varied types of chakras, predictions about natural occurrences rainfalls, earthquakes, natural disasters and epidemics, results of planetary movements on nations, masses and commodities, etc.

Astrology is a Vedanga or one of the limbs of the vedas. Vedas were studied by the ancient sages and rishis out of whom saptarishis (7 great sages) were the most celebrated. There are a number of conflicting versions on the 7 names. The names that frequent these versions are Vashista, Bharadwaja, Jamadagni, Gautama, Atri, Vishvamitra, Agastya, Kasyapa, Brighu, Angirasa, Marichi, Pulastya, Pulaha, and Kratu. Sage Bhrigu was one of the saptarishis who is also known to have been the wish-born-son of Lord Brahma.The bhrigus also known as bhargavas were a clan of sages descending from the ancient fire-priest Bhrigu. The Bhrigus are intimately linked with composition of Atharva Veda.

Sage Bhrigu is credited as the father of Hindu astrology and the first astrological treatise Bhrigu Samhita is attributed to his authorship. This treatise is said to contain over 5 million horoscopes, in which he wrote down the fate of every being in the universe. According to the popular tradition, only a handful of these horoscopes are known to have survived to this age.

Although the bhrigu samhita is an astrological classic written by Maharishi Bhrigu during the vedic period, yet the available evidence corroborates that it was compiled over a period of time by the various students of bhrigu. Bhrigu maharishi was the first compiler of predictive astrology which came to be known as the fifth veda of treta yuga. He compiled the horoscopes with the help of Lord Ganesha which formed essential database for further research. This study culminated in the birth of the science (Shastra) of determining the quality of time (Hora) known as Brihat Prasara Hora Shastra.

Maharishi Parashara's name is also synonymous with Vedic astrology and has often been quoted by modern day astrologers. Parashara was a rigvedic maharishi and is believed to have authored and/or tutored his students several ancient Indian texts. He was the grandson of Sage Vashista (one of the saptarishis) and the father of Veda Vyasa who was the author of Mahabharata. He is also credited by many as being the speaker of the Brihat Prasara Hora Shastra which is considered to be the most comprehensive extant work on Vedic astrology.

History of the Classical Planets: Classical planets are seven non-fixed visible objects in the sky. They are Sun, Moon, Mars, Mercury, Jupiter, Venus, and Saturn. Ancient astronomers termed them as being wandering stars. In vedic astrology planets are also known by the term grahas. Grahas literally means 'cosmic influencers'. Practitioners of vedic astrology claim that grahas influence the auras and minds of all beings connected to Earth by carrying and imparting a specific energy quality that each of them is associated with. Each of these classical planets was also accorded a day of the week. There are multiple versions on the history of the grahas or planets of vedic astrology. We briefly explain one such version in vogue on their creation and existence.

Surya / Ravi / Aditya (Sun): When the universe was an utterly dark sphere, Lord Brahma, the creator God, split it of the centre and the sound 'OM' reverberated. The Planet Sun is thus thought to be self-created. However, it is also stated that he was born to the sage Kasyapa and his wife Aditi.

Chandra (Moon): It is believed that Planet Moon was born out of the divine chest of Lord Vishnu. Another version states that Chandra was born in the Ocean of Milk (the gods were churning it for millennia, in order to create immortal life), and nearly blinded the gods with his bright, glowing body (hence the name that means "illustrious"). The gods unanimously decided to give Chandra the status of a planet and sent him into the cosmos.

Mangala (Mars): Mars or Mangala also goes by the name Bhauma or Angaraka. After separating from goddess Parvathi, Lord Shiva was performing penance. During this time, a drop of sweat from his forehead eye fell to the ground and assumed the form of a beautiful child with a reddish complexion. It is believed that goddess Earth nurtured and brought up the child and named him Bhauma.When Bhauma grew up, he went to Kashi and did a tremendous penance to please lord Shiva. Lord Shiva blessed him by granting him 'Mangala loka' (the Abode of Mangala). Mangala or Mars thus went onto become one of the planets.

Budha (Mercury): Budha is said to have been born to Tara and Chandra. Budha vigorously performed penance to Lord Shiva and was granted the status of a planet. In addition, he also performed penance to Lord Vishnu to master all the vedas and the arts and sciences.

Brihaspati (Jupiter): Brihaspati or Guru or Jupiter is known to be the son of Chitra Devi and Saint Angirasa (who is one of the favorite sons of Lord Brahma). He is known to be the guru or teacher to the devas. It is said that Brihaspati performed penance on the banks of Prabhas Tirtha to Lord Shiva who bestowed him the title of guru to the devas and also the status of a planet.

Shukra (Venus): It is widely believed that Shukra is the child of Bhrigu and Kiyathi. Bhrigu is one of the favorite sons of Lord Brahma. Shukra is known to be the Guru of the Asuras or demons. An alternate version states that Shukra resided and meditated inside the stomach of Lord Shiva for 1000 years. Then Lord Shiva ejected Shukra into the world as a live being. He was granted the status of a planet, because he stayed inside Lord Shiva's physical body for many years.

Shani (Saturn): Shani is known to be the son of Surya and his wife Chhaya and hence goes by the name of Chayyaputra.Shani established a Linga (a form of Lord Shiva) at Banaras and fervently prayed for long. As a result, he was accorded the status of a planet.

2

Tropical and Sidereal Astrology (Western Vs. Vedic)

We often see a difference in the dates of the 12 zodiacs or rasis (We shall examine the 12 zodiacs in detail in the next chapter) followed in western astrology and vedic or Hindu astrology. For example, as per western astrology September 5 happens to be Virgo while in vedic astrology this happens to be Leo. How does such a difference arise? The answer to this question lies in the concept of tropical and sidereal zodiacs. Let us first examine some astronomical concepts before we jump into the conclusion with regard to the difference between the two.

Ecliptic Coordinate System:

Think of an imaginary sphere with a large radius with a common centre with any celestial body. Let us term this as a celestial sphere. The apparent path of the Sun on such a celestial sphere is known as the ecliptic and is the basis for the ecliptic co-ordinate system.The **ecliptic coordinate system** or **celestial coordinate system** (A system for specifying positions of celestial or heavenly objects such as planets and stars) is used for representing the positions and orbits of heavenly bodies. Coordinate systems can specify a position in 3-dimensional space, or merely the direction of the object on the celestial sphere. It is implemented in spherical or rectangular coordinates.The spherical coordinates here are the celestial latitudes, celestial longitudes and distance. Since many planets of the solar system, including Earth have an inclination to the ecliptic, their positions are obtained using the ecliptic coordinate system.

The position of a celestial object east of the vernal equinox along the ecliptic is the celestial longitude or ecliptic longitude.

Celestial longitude is measured in degrees eastward from the vernal equinox (0°) to the point where a circle drawn through the object and the poles of the ecliptic intersects the ecliptic. The vernal equinox here represents March 21 as per Western Astrology but April 14 as per vedic astrology. Longitudes are measured in degrees with each degree (°) representing 1/360th of a circle with each degree (°) consisting of 60 minutes (') and each minute consisting of 60 seconds ("). As it is a right handed system ecliptic longitude is measured positive eastwards in the fundamental plane. Celestial latitude or ecliptic latitude measures the angular distance of an object from the ecliptic towards the north or south ecliptic pole (point on the celestial sphere where the sphere meets the imaginary line perpendicular to the ecliptic plane the path the Earth travels on its orbit around the Sun). The position of all the planets of the solar system is computed using the above system.

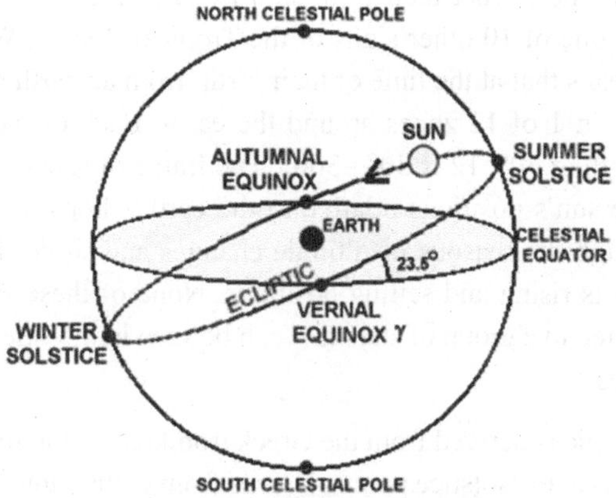

Figure 1: Celestial Sphere

The **Tropical Zodiac** is the position of the sun referenced against the earth's horizon at a particular location which gives you the seasons as a measure of the flow of time. The four seasons are defined as per the summer and winter solstices (Remember, the longest and the shortest days of the year on 21 June and 22 December?) and the spring and autumnal equinoxes (Daytime and night of equal duration on March 21 and September 23?). An equinox occurs when the plane of Earth's equator passes the center of the Sun. At that instant, the tilt of Earth's axis neither inclines away from nor towards the Sun. A solstice, of course, occurs when the Sun reaches its highest or lowest point relative to the equator. To an observer on Earth the Sun reaches its highest point in the sky on a solstice day. This is the system most **western astrologers** use. The longitude of any celestial object as per the tropical zodiac goes by the name of **Sayana Longitude**.

The **Sidereal Zodiac** is the position of the sun referenced against the star background, as a measure of the flow of time.While classical tropical astrology is based on the orientation of the Earth relative to the Sun and planets of the solar system, sidereal astrology deals with the position of the Earth relative to both of these as well as the stars of the celestial sphere. This is the system **astronomers and practitioners of Vedic astrology** put into use. The longitude of any celestial object, as per the sidereal zodiac, goes by the name of **Nirayana Longitude**.

Most people know what their birth sign is. They may be a "Leo" or a "Taurus" or one of 10 other signs of the Tropical Zodiac. What does it mean? It means that at the time of their birth, from an earth perspective, the sun was in 1 of 12 zones around the earth. Each of the 12 has an angular length of 30°. 12 X 30° =360°. The frame of reference for these zones is the sun's positions relative to the earth's horizon. As the sun moves through the seasons its altitude changes and so do the compass bearings of its rising and setting positions. None of these signs can be directly related to a group of stars that can be seen in the skies with one's physical eyes.

The word tropic is derived from the Greek tropikos - belonging to a turn. The Sun turns at the solstice points. It turns from getting lower and lower in the sky at midday (heading to midwinter) to start climbing higher and higher (heading to midsummer) and vice versa.

The sidereal zodiac uses the physical stars visible in the night sky as its frame of reference for obtaining the position of sun, moon or any planet in the sky. Generally speaking, the sidereal zodiac (as seen by a person standing on the earth) is that belt of stars 7^0 either side of the sun's path (ecliptic) through the sky that is divided into 12 equal sized (30^0) constellations. This zodiac is like a freeway with a central lane (ecliptic) on which the sun travels. The moon and planets also travel on this freeway but on different lanes. They do, however, cross each other's lanes at times (nodes). The word sidereal is derived from Latin *sidus* 'star'.

Precession of Equinoxes:

We now are aware of the fact that the sidereal zodiac defines the signs based on fixed stars while the tropical zodiac is based on the relative position of the Sun and the Earth and the concept of equinoxes.As a result of the Earth's orientation or axial tilt there is a difference in the dates of both these zodiacs. This is explained by the concept of Precession of Equinoxes. The word precession indicates a change in the orientation of the rotational axis of a rotating body. The earth is spherical and rotates from west to east around its axis. Its orbit around the Sun is elliptical. The axis of the earth is an imaginary line which, passing through its centre, connects its two poles, the north pole and the south pole. Another imaginary line running across the largest circumference of the earth, equidistant from its poles and running in an east-west direction, is called the equator.

We have already touched upon the concept of the equinoxes while studying tropical zodiacs. When the Sun is passing from the southern hemisphere to the northern hemisphere, it cuts the equator at vernal equinox. When the division of the circle of the zodiac is with reference to vernal equinox as its starting point, the zodiac is referred to as the Sayana (or tropical) zodiac, the divisions of this zodiac into twelve equal parts are the Sayana rasis, and the positions of planets in this zodiac represent the Sayana longitudes of the planets.

If we could watch the sky for a few hundred years, we would discover that the north celestial pole is moving slowly with respect to Dhruva or pole star. The celestial poles and the celestial equator, which are supposed to be the fixed reference marks, are moving very slowly because of the slow change in the direction of Earth's axis of rotation. This slow top-like motion is called precession. Earth's axis sweeps around in a cone, taking almost 26,000 years for each sweep.The vernal equinox itself precesses slowly westward relative to the fixed stars, completing one revolution in about 26,000 years.

Precession is caused by the gravitational pull of the Sun and the Moon. Because earth is not a perfect sphere – it has a slight bulge around its equator – Sun and Moon pull on it, trying to make it spin upright in its orbit. This forces earth's axis to precess. The result of this precession is that vernal equinox, the cutting point of the ecliptic and the celestial equator, drifts westward on the ecliptic by an approximate angle of 50.3 seconds of an arc each year. So we have a new vernal equinox every year and, hence, a new staring point of the Sayana zodiac. This results in the shifting of the Sayana signs.

It is of decisive importance to remember that the Vedic system does not depend upon this shifting zodiac and relies upon a fixed point on the zodiac as its starting point. When the division of the circle of the zodiac is with reference to the Vedic starting point, the zodiac is referred to as the Nirayana (or Sidereal) zodiac, the twelve equal parts are the Nirayana rasis, and the positions of planets in this zodiac represent the Nirayana longitudes of the planets.

Ayanamsa:

The Sanskrit word Ayanamsa is made up of Ayana meaning "Movement" and Amsa meaning "Component". It is a Sanskrit term for the amount of precession. Mathematically, it is the difference between the Nirayana (Sidereal) and Sayana (Tropical) longitude. In astronomy, too, this is the difference between the length of a tropical year (365.2422 rotations of the earth) and a sidereal year (365.2563 rotations) required to complete one orbit relative to the sun (tropical) or stars (sidereal).

Ayanamsa = Sayana (Tropical) Longitude – Nirayana (Sidereal) Longitude

There are quite a few versions for the number that is to be used for obtaining the Ayanamsa but the most popular one is the Chitrapaksha Ayanamsa which takes into account Chitra nakshatra or constellation as the base of the zodiac. It is said to be the brightest constellation as per the surya siddhanta (classical text on astronomy) and the center of this nakshatra is exactly opposite or 180 degrees opposite the 1st zodiac of Aries. It also goes by the name of Lahiri Ayanamsa. Prof. N.C.Lahiri is said to have popularized this ayanamsa technique. Most Indian almanacs follow the Lahiri Ayanamsa.

For the year 2000 Lahiri Ayanamsa is assumed to be 23.85 degrees.

Ayanamsa increases by approximately 1.4 degrees (1 degree and 24 minutes) arc per century or approximately 50.3 seconds every year.

One formula that could be used for obtaining Lahiri Ayanamsa is

A = 23:51:23 + 50.291" * t + 1.11161" * T

Here 23°51′23″ (23 degrees, 51 minutes and 23 seconds) represents the Ayanamsa value on 1/1/2000, it is the number of years since 2000 (negative if year is less than 2000) and T is the number of centuries of 36525 days from 2000.

Example 1:

Calculate the Ayanamsa value for 15th August, 2014.

Applying the above formula we get

t = 14.621918 (August 15 is 227th day of 2014)

T = 0.146229 (August 15th marks the 5341th day since the start of century)

A = 23:51:23 + 50.291 * 14.621918 + 1.11161 * 0.146229

Or

A = 24:3:39 (24°3'39")(24 degrees, 3 minutes and 39 seconds)

Sidereal Day vs Solar Day:

We use clocks or wristwatches to tell the time of the day. These times are based on standard time zones set by various nations. They are primarily based on the movement of the Sun in the sky during the course of a day. A solar day is the time it takes for the Earth to rotate about its axis so that the Sun appears in the same position in the sky. A sidereal day is the time it takes for the Earth to rotate about its axis so that the distant stars appear in the same position in the sky. The sidereal day is --4 minutes shorter than the solar day. A clock that is regulated by the movement of the stars in the sky is a sidereal clock. Astronomers use such time keeping instruments.

One earth day consists of 24 hours and there are 365.2422 days in a year on average (including the leap year and century). During this one year period earth makes a complete revolution around the Sun. If we look at from the perspective of the stars in the sky one complete revolution equals 360 degrees or a complete circle or the time it would take to make a complete revolution with respect to a fixed star in the sky. Thus a sidereal day would be faster than a solar day by 360 degrees / 365.2422 or 1/365.2422 or 24 * 365.2422/366.2422 or a sidereal day is equal to 23 hours 56 minutes and 4 seconds. Thus a sidereal day is faster than a solar day by 4 minutes. This means that a particular star will rise 4 minutes earlier every night, and is the reason why different constellations are only visible at specific times of the year. A tropical year is equal to 365d 5h 48m 46s while a sidereal year is 365d 6h 9m 9.5s.

Table 1: Tropical and Sidereal Dates (Position of Sun in 12 Zodiacs)

Zodiac	Tropical Dates	Sidereal Dates
Aries (Mesha)	March 21 - April 20	April 14 - May 14
Taurus (Vrishaba)	April 21 - May 21	May 15 - June 14
Gemini (Mithuna)	May 22 - June 21	June 15 - July 15
Cancer (Kataka)	June 22 - July 22	July 16 - August 16
Leo (Simha)	July 23 - August 22	August 17 – September 16
Virgo (Kanya)	August 23 - September 23	September 17 - October 16
Libra (Tula)	September 24 - October 23	October 17 - November 15
Scorpio (Vrischika)	October 24 - November 22	November 16 - December 15
Sagittarius (Dhanus)	November 23 - December 21	December 16 - January 13
Capricorn (Makara)	December 22 - January 20	January 14 - February 12
Aquarius (Kumbha)	January 21 - February 19	February 13 - March 14
Pisces (Meena)	February 20 - March 20	March 15 - April 13

Note: Dates may vary according to the year on account of Precession of Equinoxes.

3

12 Zodiacs or Rasis

Astrologically speaking, the zodiac is a circle of twelve 30° divisions of celestial longitude that are centered upon the ecliptic. The paths of the Moon and visible planets also remain close to the ecliptic, within the belt of the zodiac, which extends 8-9° north or south of the ecliptic, as measured in celestial latitude.

Historically, these twelve divisions are called signs. Essentially, the zodiac is an ecliptic coordinate system, which takes the ecliptic as the origin of latitude, and the position of the sun at vernal equinox as the origin of longitude.

The Sanskrit word for Zodiac is 'Rashi' or 'Rasi' which is composed of two halves "Ra" indicating Rahu or the Northern Lunar Node and "Shi" which is one of the names of Ketu or the southern lunar node. These 12 rasis indicate the material creation which governs our lives. The intuition behind there being 12 rasis comes from the fact that there are 12 conjunctions (New Moon) and oppositions (Full Moon) of the Sun and Moon in a calendar year and that it takes 30 days on average for such a phenomenon to occur. Maharishi Parashara has stated that the 12 rasis are the limbs of the supreme lord Maha Vishnu and their order goes by the term Kalapurusha. These twelve rasis beginning from mesha represent the head, face, arms, heart, stomach, hips, and space below navel, the private parts, thighs, knees, ankles and feet of the Kalapurusha. Kalapurusha means time eternal or time personified. On any given day each of the 12 rasis rise in the eastern horizon of the sky at intervals of approximately once in 2 hours (12 signs * 2 hours = 24 hours). The order varies based on the month of the year.

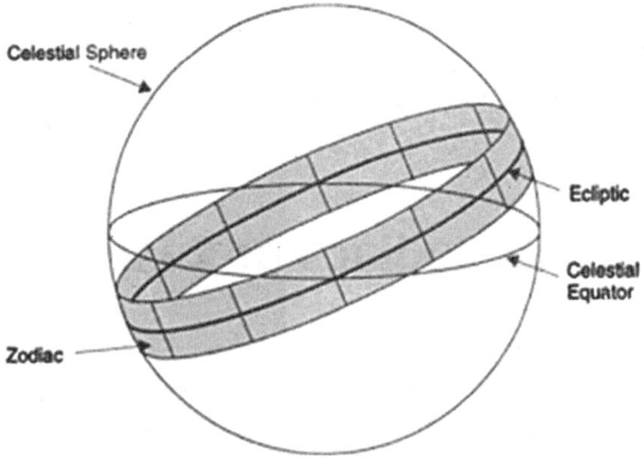

Figure 2: Zodiac Belt

Following is the list of 12 zodiacs / rasis and certain characteristics associated with them:-

Table 2: Zodiacs and Rasis

Zodiac	Rasi	Planetary Ruler	Division of the Zodiac
Aries	Mesha	Mars	0 to 30°
Taurus	Vrishaba	Venus	30 to 60°
Gemini	Mithuna	Mercury	60 to 90°
Cancer	Kataka	Moon	90 to 120°
Leo	Simha	Sun	120 to 150°
Virgo	Kanya	Mercury	150 to 180°
Libra	Tula	Venus	180 to 210°
Scorpio	Vrischika	Mars	210 to 240°
Sagittarius	Dhanus	Jupiter	240 to 270°
Capricorn	Makara	Saturn	270 to 300°
Aquarius	Kumbha	Saturn	300 to 330°

Aries (Mesha):

Aries is the first astrological sign in the Zodiac, spanning the first 30 degree of the zodiac. Under the tropical zodiac, the Sun transits this sign between March 21 and April 20 each year. Under the sidereal zodiac, the sun currently transits Aries from 14 April to 14 May (approximately).

Its symbol is the Ram. It is a cardinal fire male sign. Mesha or Aries is the first sign of the Rasichakra. The appearance is like a lamb and holds a position right at the head of the Kalapurusha. People born under this sign are primarily doers and are devoid of malice and fear. Their bravery and courage can often lead them to the point of foolishness. They are impetuous, head-strong and spontaneous in their expressions and actions and can also be self-centered in their attitude. These people have strong leadership qualities and are always eager to make their presence felt through words or actions. They hate compromising with their desires and can go to any extent in attaining and fulfilling their wishes. Mesha people have this innate tendency to react physically to everything. They literally tend to ram their way into the matter whenever they are out to attain any of their wants. They usually lack the patience to reason out the situation and the pros and the cons and simply deal with a situation impulsively given their emotional and passionate nature. People around them often feel flattered by this rash behavior but when it borders on extreme recklessness, they can even be a big turn off. The Meshas also forget their frustrations and anger pretty soon. The Meshas participate with great gusto in the everyday activities of life. Their highly spirited and optimistic nature makes them very active and fiery in all their endeavors. They are athletic and energetic and can make friends pretty easily. As they have good leadership qualities, they are charismatic and courageous. Similarly, in spite of the fact that the Meshas have excellent potential to be good leaders, they are not always able to attain the mission that they had set out for. Their impulsiveness comes in the way to judge a given situation effectively and rationally and take appropriate decisions. Though they are high on physical energy, they require persistent stimulation. When they are unable to find it, they might well turn lethargic.

Taurus (Vrishaba):

Taurusis the second astrological sign in the Zodiac. It spans the 30-60th degree of the zodiac. Under the tropical zodiac, the Sun transits this sign on average between April 21 and May 21 each year. Under the sidereal zodiac, the sun currently transits Taurus from May 15 to June 14 (approximately). Its symbol is the bull. It is a fixed earth female sign. People born under the Vrishaba rasi are calm and stable people who are dependable and are confident of reaching their goal in life. At times perceived to be stubborn, they are extremely humane in their approach towards situations and people alike. And they cannot accept anything less than what they believe they deserve. They are very determined individuals. They are able to focus on their goals and decide on their course of actions through determination and constant observation. They are good planners and arrive at a decision after due consideration of all the relevant factors. They are more concerned about the simple and functional aspects of life as they seek stability in all their actions and planning. This makes them pretty conventional in their approach towards everyday situations. They avoid taking unprecedented or unconventional approach in life and they are seldom experimental with new ideas or thoughts. This constant penchant for stability and simplicity often comes across as boring to others, but they are least willing to change for the whims and fancies of others. The Vrishaba is not prone to taking unnecessary risks and end up falling into some jeopardy where, he can easily place himself in a solid footing. Since the key planet of the vrishaba is Venus, the symbol of love and desire, people born under this zodiac sign are aware of the satisfaction of the senses and are sensual. In spite of being perpetually pragmatic, they feel that it is also necessary to take care of the senses. They find material and pleasure giving things as appealing. This makes them prefer comfortable living, good ambience and soothing workplace. They are also in quest of the beauty that lies beyond the material possessions, that is, they are aware of mystic and the spiritual. This also explains their relentless desire for ideal love in comparison to physical love. Since this rasi has the earth as the principle element, the Vrishaba is supposed to be naturally practical. Their perception of life is based more on reality and pragmatism than on fiction and fantasy. Whenever they are apprehensive, they seek advice and arrive at decisions only after serious thoughtful consideration. Seeing is believing for these people who are very possessive. They treasure everything that they belong to them. They are extremely concerned about their personal possessions and even the immaterial things hold great personal value for them.

Gemini (Mithuna):

Gemini is the third astrological sign in the Zodiac, spanning the 60th-90th degree of the zodiac. Under the tropical zodiac, the sun transits this sign between May 22 and June 21. Under the sidereal zodiac, the sun currently transits Gemini from June 15 to July 15 (approximately).Its symbol is the gemini twins. It is a mutable air male sign. Gemini or Mithuna is symbolization of dual nature. The opposites play a very easy and natural role in their character. People born under this rasi can like things that are totally opposite in nature. A Mithuna can be curious and garrulous at the same time and be extremely versatile with a high mental alacrity on the other. They are highly likable in the light-hearted social encounters as this attitude of prancing through topics is welcome for the casual get-togethers. Most people consider the company of Mithuna as fun, but then they are also perceived to be shallow and fickle minded. Mithunas have a razor sharp wit. They take their own time in making decisions. They avoid flying speedily and indulge in rash decisions. They smell the flowers before actually buying a bouquet. The key planet of the Mithuna is mercury. It is the planet of childhood and youth. This in fact explains the manner in which the Mithuna communicates its inner feelings and thoughts. They have a rational mind and are usually alert to their situations and react accordingly in given conditions. Communication is also one of the important aspects of the Mithuna character which is a key element in relationships as in the interaction they have with the people around them which is very jovial. Communication also symbolizes the short distance travel and trips for the Mithuna. But what comes across as whimsicalness or fickle-mindedness is actually the impatience that is symbolized by its key planet mercury. Movement in thought and action is natural air or vayu is the principle element of the Mithuna. It symbolizes eternal movement. This also greatly explains their character, the fact that they are prone to make alterations in their thoughts and actions. Since they have an alert mind, they have an excellent command over language. Mithuna individuals are articulate and great communicators and good thinkers as well. They give a lot of importance to their intellect.

Cancer (Kataka):

Cancer is the fourth astrological sign and spans the 90-120th degree of the zodiac. Under the tropical zodiac, the Sun transits this sign on an average between June 22 and July 22, and under the sidereal zodiac, the Sun transits this sign between approximately July 16 and August 16. Its symbol is the crab. It is a cardinal water female sign. The hard outer shell that protects the crab acts for a similar purpose for the Kataka Rasi (Karka Rasi) people as well. The external hardness is their defense that is confined to just the outer shell. The individual is otherwise extremely sensitive from within. Their sensitivity can cause them to hold their feelings and not come out with their emotions. Crabs have clinching claws that they actually indicate the manner in which the kataka native is prone to holding on to things that are often related to their past. The biggest strength of a kataka native is his/her ability to nurture. These individuals are passionately loyal and they just cannot let go easily. They are also very prompt and eager to bring their loved ones under the proverbial protection of their outer shell. They can protect with all their might and bears all the difficulties willingly, just to ensure the comfort of the people who seek their shelter or help. If the anger resulting from the inability to do something effective builds up for a long time, there can be symptoms of resentment and depression. There is also this desire to find someone with whom the Kataka is able to trust and share his feelings. The defensiveness is a mode for offense for the Kataka. Just as the crab baits its prey into its territory and then attacks and overpowers it, the Kataka also lures in the person it wishes to dominate by luring the person into his domain. In a certain argument, people can think that the Kataka has retreated, but more often than not it can be a preparation for aggression. The ruling planet of the Kataka is the moon. It holds the fulcrum of the feelings and emotions and the fact that the moon keeps on changing as in, the moon is never same for two consecutive nights. This thereby also brings them closer to the subconscious realm of the moon. Since nurturing is the primary characteristic of the Kataka, they can make very good mothers. The primary element of the Kataka is water. The Flow of Water is deep and ceaseless. Just as the cycle of water is never-ending, emotions are also never-ending for the Kataka. The feelings likewise have a constant flow as they act as a connection of the present and the past experiences of the Kataka's life.

Leo (Simha):

Leo is the fifth astrological sign of the zodiac. It spans the 120-150th degree of the Tropical zodiac. Under the tropical zodiac, the Sun transits this sign on an average between July 23 and August 22 each year, and under the sidereal zodiac, the sun currently transits this sign from approximately August 17 to September 16. Its symbol is the Lion. It is a fixed fire male sign. The characteristics of the persons belonging to Simha Rasi are very akin to a lion. They exhibit an air of loyalty. They are prone to choose an action or behave in a manner that puts them in the limelight. They always crave for acknowledgment and appreciation and love to be the centre of attraction in any given gathering. And the need for approval is the Simha's greatest weakness. A Simha is always prepared to act; they love to indulge in things that others will also appreciate. They have this relentless desire to be loved for the good that they are doing to others. The Simha can prove to be a total paradoxical character. They have the potential to be a high-minded leader and they are a very faithful servant as well. This trait flows down to their relationship status, too. A Simha is very straight forward in the manner that he leads his life. They are always honest in their approach and it is interesting to note that they have a flair for show-off and drama. This naturally follows the trait observed in the lion. Just as the king of the jungle loves appreciation and the aura that surrounds him, a Simha also craves for attention. The Simha is often found to be attracted to the theatre or anything that is related to performing arts and public relations. This is because they love to meet people and make new connections. Although they relish being hailed for their achievements, the Simha also does not overlook the sentiments of people who are around them. They are concerned about the well being and the feelings of the people who are attached to them. The Simha gets his/her trait from its key planet the Sun. Just as the sun is the king of the planetary system, the Simha also revels in being hailed as the most important person around. They have a strong will that acts as the energy that keeps the desire in the furnaces burning. It is this that acts as a motivation to live. The principal element of this rasi is fire. A Simha lives on his own energy regardless of the requirement of the situation. A fire lives in the moment; likewise, a Simha relies upon his intuition and survival instincts, in order to live his life. The brilliance and intensity of the energy of the Simha is pretty high.

Virgo (Kanya):

Virgo is the sixth astrological sign in the Zodiac. It spans the 150-180th degree of the zodiac. Under the tropical zodiac, the Sun transits this sign on an average between August 23 and September 23, and under the sidereal zodiac, the sun currently transits Virgo from September 17 to October 16. Its symbol is the virgin maiden. It is a mutable earth female sign. Discrimination and focus are the two attributes that characterize the Kanya native. The manner in which they deal with their personal desires, gives an insight into their character. They can deal with a situation with a laser-like focus while at the same time, there can be a marked prudishness in their passion. The Kanya can be a brutal critic. Such an individual can be exceptionally critical as a judge and can instantly decide on what is wrong. This is true in relation to a given person, situation or environment. Their sense of judgment is their greatest asset, and criticism comes to them naturally. Their mental process does not have a very creative bent but they are often rescued from the most challenging and the trickiest of situations due to their razor-sharp thinking ability. They know how to dissociate the materials that are not worthwhile from those that are really necessary. They know how to differentiate between the good and the bad. These people also have a persistent desire to be perfect in all their actions. They strive for becoming perfect. Performance and efficiency is very important to them. The Kanya can also be very fastidious. Since they cannot be satisfied so easily, they can often find themselves in a situation where they end up limiting their interactions and experiences even before they actually take place. People around them often feel that kanya natives can become better companions if they are able to be less severe in their criticisms, whether pertaining to themselves or others. This character trait of being overtly critical somehow lies in the fact that the key planet of the Kanya is mercury, the planet that symbolizes our thoughts and the manner in which they get expressed. Mercury also takes care of the language house. The Kanya critically analyses every bit of information that enters his mind. Since the key element of the Kanya is Earth, they are seldom found to resort in fantasy. They always have their feet firmly on the ground. Their basic sensibilities make them excellent critics and, therefore, good advisors as well. Thoughts and feelings are often found to take a back seat with the Kanya. Practicality is their forte.

Libra (Tula):

Libra is the seventh astrological sign in the Zodiac. It spans the 180-210th degree of the zodiac. Under the tropical zodiac, Sun transits this sign on an average between (northern autumnal equinox) September 24 and October 23, and under the sidereal zodiac, the sun currently transits Libra from approximately October 17 to November 15. Its symbol is the scales. It is a cardinal air male sign. An individual born under the Tula rasi is considered to be the most sociable of all the signs. The tula falls midway between a human and an animal. They look forward to putting others at ease and so their response to situations is quite graceful. They are pretty inclined to arts and they are adept in striking a perfect balance between form, color and element. This makes them choose creative fields. The Tula is famous for his/her ability to balance. The manner in which he/she manages to align the schedule between himself/herself and others calls for appreciation. Be it a social act or the intricacies of an inter-personal relationship, the Tula is always a winner. The Tula can have excellent intuitive qualities. They have this unique ability to intuitively understand what the person before them might possibly ask for. They are concerned and give due importance to the requirements of others and take great care in fulfilling their expectations. Since they are adept in gauging, understanding and complying with the expectations of people, they are great negotiators as well. They work on all available options, in order to arrive at the right one. They go for solutions that are mutually acceptable for all concerned. This attribute also leads to the fact that the Tulas are great as strategists, too. They can negotiate to the satisfaction of all the parties and their understanding of the cause and effect relationship is also great. They are experts in traveling by the middle path. The key planet of the Tula is Venus. Therefore, love, desire, romance and beauty are aspects that the Tula will be more focused on. Art and painting are their main forte and they are prone to perceive beauty as ideal. The principle element of the Tula is air. Air symbolizes movement. Between two given points, it is the thought that has the most effectual movement. This is precisely the reason that the Tula is able to decide and judge between two options. As it travels back and forth, it is able to judge the pros and cons and, therefore, zero in on the best alternative. They give due importance to intellect and this add on to the attribute. Then, people who are born under the air sign are excellent communicators.

Scorpio (Vrischika):

Scorpio is the eighth astrological sign in the Zodiac. It spans the 210-240th degree of the zodiac. Under the tropical zodiac, the sun transits this sign on an average between October 24 and November 22, and under the sidereal zodiac, the sun currently transits Scorpio from approximately November 16 to December 15. Its symbol is the scorpion. It is a fixed water female sign. There is this myth that people should better be careful while dealing with vrischikas. The most remarkable quality about the vrischika's character is that their tendency to use their strong emotional awareness to make their opponent or attacker harmless. The principal strength of the Vrischika is the passion they have for their feelings, while the most important weakness is their propensity to secrecy. Vrischika has this unique ability to cause transformation of the painful scorpion poison into a level of higher consciousness that thrives on universal love. The hidden element of the Vrischika happens to be the most interesting and alluring aspect of his character. Most of the Vrischikas are found to have an attractive personality that pulls people towards them. This is the fact that causes them to have a lot of followers, thereby making them good leaders. If the Vrischikas happen to get scorned in love, they can well turn utterly cold and withdrawn. The tendency towards the matters lying underneath our consciousness is so appealing to a vrischika individual. Vrischikas are thus often found to be attracted to things that others do not or may not really understand. The hidden power in the Vrischikas is also a matter of profound concern. The sexual issue in the Vrischika involves another person in the life of the Vrischika. Then there is the final transformation that is Death. This may not mean the death of the individual himself. Water is the principal element in the Vrischika. And water is associated with emotion. This entails that, at times, when the emotions are deep, just like the depth of waters, the Vrischika find it difficult to put them down in words. Then the cycle is also endless as the cycle of water.

Sagittarius (Dhanus):

Sagittarius is the ninth astrological sign. It spans the 240–270th degree of the zodiac. Under the tropical zodiac, the sun transits this sign on an average between November 23 and December 21, and under the sidereal zodiac, the sun currently transits Sagittarius from December 16 to January 13. Its symbol is the archer. It is a mutable fire male sign. The Dhanus native is an incurable optimist. They can see a possibility even in the most improbable of situations. This is actually symbolized by the arrow of thought that is always pointed upwards. They always tend to look at the brighter side of the life and even encourage others to do the same. It is also an interesting aspect to note that the Dhanus's honesty lands them in a soup almost to the point of being a fault. The Dhanus can prove to be a very good companion. They are usually outgoing and extrovert and prefer to stay in a cheerful mood. This makes them likable by all but, if they happen to feel dominated by anyone, they rebel and stubborn. They love their own independence and like to enjoy life in its own pace. Clipping the wings of a dhanus native can turn them into a completely different individual. They are frank and outspoken and out right honest in their approach; and this continues in the manner in which they express themselves, too. They speak out their mind regarding others without even realizing that this might hurt the feelings of the person before him at that instant. The Dhanus loves to ride. They enjoy sports a lot and find outdoor sports like hiking, trekking and even running very exciting. The Dhanus is a seeker of knowledge and wisdom. If they feel themselves restricted, they use their knowledge and try to seek out options. They are eternally hopeful. This basically acts as an inspiration that helps them to attain success. The key planet Jupiter helps the dhanus native to see even the smallest of opportunities to appear larger than life. The Jupiter acts as a sort of magnifying glass and, as it were, serves as an optical projector. The Dhanus ends up taking life as an adventure and they carry conviction in something that is greater than themselves. Since it is the largest planet of our solar system, Jupiter acts as a representation of expansive action. This makes Dhanus love the big, the best and the infinite. This acts as a pointer to the next aspect of Dhanus. As it is never always right to have anything too much, the Dhanus actually falls prey to the natural characteristic of Jupiter, to overspend and over indulge. The key element of the Dhanus is fire. It never faces depletion and continuously gives light and heat. It allows others to feed on its warmth. The Dhanus is unpredictable just as the fire is not itself aware of its next move. It lives in the moment and burns itself in the available fuel without any forethought. It is the instinct for, and the intuition to, survival that it solely relies on. The most positive attribute of the fire in the Dhanus native is that it is warming and not hot. This is explained by the fact that the Jupiter is far off from the sun. The fire acts more as a direction provider and source of inspiration that motivates the mind to reach out to the hitherto unexplored wilderness around.

Capricorn (Makara):

Capricorn is the tenth astrological sign in the zodiac. It spans the 270–300th degree of the zodiac. Under the tropical zodiac, the sun transits this sign from December 22 to January 20 each year, and under the sidereal zodiac, the sun currently transits Capricorn from approximately January 14 to February 12. Its symbol is the goat. It is a cardinal earth female sign. The Makara is represented by the goat. Since the goat can climb to higher altitudes better than any other mammal, the Makara usually sets higher goals for himself/herself. They are more efficient in overcoming the obstructions that lie between themselves and their destination, that is, the personal mountain that exists on their road to success. The Makara native is very conscious about his/her status. He/she gives a lot of importance to whether those surrounding him/her are giving due respect to him/her. This adulation basically adds to their personal satisfaction and is as dear to them as their achievements. The Makara is very impulsive at times. But more often than not his/her actions are actually preplanned. This is a bit of a paradoxical attitude. Before deciding upon something, they spend a fair amount of time thinking on the consequences of their actions and then decide whether to at all go ahead with it. The Makara is usually conservative in his/her approach to life and expressions. Their experimentation is limited to what they might require to attain their goal. They have a lot of confidence in their abilities and believe that the course they have taken will sure reach them to their coveted destination. The key planet of Makara is Saturn. Limitation is a key characteristic of Saturn. Here there is a positive linkage to the spiritual practice as well. The importance of this practice in life is that it helps one to reap the benefits later in the form of attainment of satisfaction that is defined by something that is beyond material pleasures. Similarly, the Makara is liable to be rewarded by the superior wisdom due to its single minded perseverance. The key planet Saturn also ensures that the Makara native gets what he/she actually deserves. Their life chart usually marks the statement that integrity and hard work pays off well. The Makara is also a strong career minded person. Work and profession holds an important place in their lives. This also explains that fact that they are deeply concerned about all that are perceived by the outer world on them. The value that they give to status and recognition also follows from here. The principal element of the Makara is earth. This symbolizes their grounded nature. They are always guided by reality and do not fancy fantasy. Imagination never controls their impulses and things that are realistic and practical only govern their life. They hold sensation dearer than feelings. Their basic sensibility is, therefore, on them pretty strong. This also explains why they are most sought after when people around them are in a dilemma and seek help to zero in on the right option. This attribute also makes them to be good founders and builders, too.

Aquarius (Kumbha):

Aquarius is the eleventh astrological sign in the Zodiac. It spans the 300° to 330° of the zodiac. Under the tropical zodiac, the sun is in Aquarius typically between January 21 and February 19, while under the Sidereal Zodiac, the sun is in Aquarius from approximately February 13 to March 14. Its symbol is the water bearer. It is a fixed air male sign. The Kumbha native is considered as the universal man, the water bearer. It is also the representation of the community of mankind. Just as the flow of water is uncontrollable, similarly the ideas that originate from the Kumbha mind are unbridled. This makes the kumbha an intellectual. The Kumbha always finds ideas and concepts very appealing. They enjoy when they are engaged in something that stimulates their intellect and they are always in a working mode. They are found to be quite laid back in their expression of their personal emotions. They are rather exceptional and unusual in their expressions. They are considered to be excellent communicators. They require to be rendered free to operate in their mental realms and this actually brings out the best in them. They have a good command over languages. This makes them friendly towards others but due to their unconventional way of expressing their feelings they, at times, find it difficult to explain how important relationships are to them. They value relationships but their inherent discomfort in expressing their feelings end up making people misunderstand their true intent and purport when they comment something unawares. Hope, dreams and friends are very important to the Kumbha.

The Kumbha is very spirited. Just as the flow of water cannot be determined, the kumbha might display an erratic behavior at one moment and be very fantastic and chilled out in another. At times, they land up in trouble due to their eccentricity. Their hidden tensions get released all of a sudden and the immediacy of the turn of events might well leave everyone spellbound.There is a positive side to them in the sense that it greatly encourages the individual to strive and win against the injustices affecting him/her. The freedom of expression that is so dear to them can be readily regained through relentless pursuit.

Pisces (Meena):

Pisces is the twelfth astrological sign in the Zodiac. It spans the 330° to 360° of the zodiac. Under the tropical zodiac the sun transits this sign on an average between February 20 and March 20 and under the sidereal zodiac, the sun transits this sign between approximately March 15 and April 13. Its symbol is fish. It is a mutable water female sign. The strength and weakness of the Meena native is his intuition and imagination at the same time. While expressing their thoughts they tend to get very emotional and they also have a deep spiritual angle into their character. The mystical aspect of everyday happenings and all other things those are present in the universe appeal to the Meena a lot. They love to dwell in the realm of their imagination and this entails their potential risk of falling apart. They end up floundering due to the absence of a solid foundation of reality. The Meena can attain salvation by offering their mystically empowered assistance to the less fortunate people who are entangled in the web of mystical confusions or desires. They can suggest them a good path by presenting a spiritual pursuit that is creatively designed to suit their needs and interest alike. They are largely dependent upon their intuitive powers and imagination to offer help and directions as they pass though the shadowy world or reality. It is an interesting aspect to note that the Meena's senses are everything that lies beyond the purview of what we commonly perceive with our five senses. This naturally follows from the above that the Meena is all about three important attributes– spirit, surrender and secret. The Meena is very emotional; this is in reference to the key element of the rasi, that is, water. Just as the unending cycle of water, the flow of emotions acts as a never ending connection between the past and the present experiences.

The manner in which the water can run very deep at certain points, the emotions of the Meena at times swell up to such a level that the profound emotion cannot be expressed in words. It is the water of consciousness, the sea of thought, feeling and belief. When connected, they naturally acquire a form that goes beyond the rational understanding of reality.

Table 3: Element and Modality of Rasis

	Fire	Earth	Air	Water
Cardinal	Mesha	Makara	Tula	Kataka
Fixed	Simha	Vrishaba	Kumbha	Vrischika
Mutable	Dhanus	Kanya	Mithuna	Meena

Elements of Astrology:

Fire: Fire is the element of creation and is thus the most active and consuming energy of the zodiac. People born under a fire sign are spontaneous and act on impulse and intuition and apply their energies wholeheartedly. Their emotional response is quick and they have a lively imagination.

Earth: Earth is a security conscious element and the most practical among the four. Earthy people react quietly and slowly. They apply themselves with endurance. Emotionally they are deeply rooted and slow to change.

Air: Air is the most intellectual and innovative element. It is unconcerned with the material side of life and is driven by a desire to communicate and share thought. Airy people are quick and animated. They apply their energies in very diverse ways and are full of novel ideas and new possibilities. They tend to intellectualize their feelings and expectations.

Water: Water is the most subtle and sensitive of elements. This is the least outwardly aware of the elements and the most irrational. People with a strongly emphasized water element are very sensitive as water is connected with feeling, cycles and fluctuations. Their imaginative and emotional lives are deep and rich.

Modalities of Astrology:

Cardinal (Movable): The 4 cardinal signs are Aries (Mesha), Cancer (Kataka), Libra (Tula) and Capricorn (Makara). Cardinal sign people have an urge to take the lead and shape things. They are initiators and act according to their aims and goals. Cardinal signs are also known as Movable signs in traditional astrology as it is during these zodiacs we witness a change in seasons. The start of Aries (Mar 21) as per tropical zodiac sees the beginning of spring or vernal equinox in the northern hemisphere and autumn in the southern hemisphere. The start of Cancer (Jun 21) sees the beginning of summer in the northern hemisphere and winter in the southern hemisphere. The start of Libra (Sep 23) sees the beginning of autumn (Autumnal Equinox) in the northern hemisphere andspring in the southern hemisphere. Finally, the onset of Capricorn (Dec 22) sees the beginning of winter in the northern hemisphere and summer in the southern hemisphere. Similarly, as per the sidereal zodiac system, the start of Capricorn or Makara (Jan 14) marks the beginning of the sun's northward journey which occurs on Makara Sankranti day or Uttarayan. The start of Kataka or Cancer (July 16) or Dakshinayan marks the beginning of sun's southward journey.

Fixed: The 4 fixed signs are Taurus (Vrishaba), Leo (Simha), Scorpio (Vrischika) and Aquarius (Kumbha). People with an emphasis on the fixed signs have a desire to build on what is already there and to organize it more efficiently. They tend to preserve a "status quo" and act in response to given circumstances. The months of the fixed signs are marked by seasonal stability.

Mutable (Dual or Common): The 4 mutable signs are Gemini (Vrishaba), Virgo (Kanya), Sagittarius (Dhanus) and Pisces (Meena). People with an emphasis on the mutable or common signs tend to seek change and renewal. They can easily replace one thing with another and align their actions with unfolding processes. Mutable signs exhibit the qualities of both Movable and Fixed signs.

Interpreting Element and Modality: Classic astrology classifies the 12 rasis or zodiacs on the basis of both their element and modality. So how does one go about finding specific differences between any 2 rasis? Kumbha rasi or Aquarius is a fixed air sign and thus will exhibit qualities of its modality such as stubbornness/inflexibility in its quest to maintain status quo. Additionally, as per its elemental classification of air it exhibits innovation and intellect. Although Aquarians, thus, are driven by novelty, yet they could desire to maintain status quo and consolidate and execute on existing norms. Contrast this with another air sign Tula rasi or Libra wh3ich will exhibit similar novelty but will have an uninhibited desire to take leadership and devise a strategy on such ideas.

Ascension of Rasis

Rasimana (Oblique Ascension): We have now studied the characteristics of natives born under any of the above 12 zodiacs or rasis. Let us now turn our attention to some arithmetic associated with these rasis. Each of the 12 rasis rises in the eastern horizon of the sky based on a particular order. One would assume that the rising period for the 12 rasis would be equal; but, nevertheless, this is not the case.Given that for the Earth the plane of the ecliptic is inclined at an angle of ~24° to the plane of the celestial equator the rising periods of the 12 rasis vary based on the latitude of the location on Earth. This inclination means that even at the equator there is a minor variation in their rising periods.

Rasimana is the term the used to describe the rising periods of the 12 signs of the zodiac. Rasimana is critical to casting a horoscope. It must be noted that Rasimana numbers are given for the **Sayana or Tropical System** and using the Ayanamsa we arrive at the Nirayana equivalent.

The following table provides the rising periods for the 12 signs at the **Equator**.

Table 4: Rasimana of Rasis at Equator

Group	Rasis				Rasimana (Asus*)	Rasimana (Hours)
I	Aries	Virgo	Libra	Pisces	1674	1h51m36s
II	Taurus	Leo	Scorpio	Aquarius	1795	1h59m40s
III	Gemini	Cancer	Sagittarius	Capricorn	1931	2h08m44s

Note: 1 Asu = 4 Seconds.

Charakhandas (Variation in Ascension): The above table provides the rising periods of the 12 signs at the Equator. Variations in the rising of different rasis, at different latitudes, can be calculated with the help of Charakhandas or ascensional variation for those latitudes. (See Appendix 1 for Charakhandas at different latitudes).

Long and Short Ascension: We have touched upon equinoxes and solstices and the variation in day and night on such days.

For people living in the northern hemisphere of the earth, on the day of winter solstice, when the Sun is at zero degrees Sayana Capricorn, the sunshine hours are the shortest. With the rising of the Sun, sign Capricorn rises in the eastern horizon followed by other signs in sequence. At the time of sunset, the point rising at the eastern horizon would be 180° opposite the Sun's longitude (thus zero degrees Cancer). Therefore, during the daytime signs Capricorn to Gemini rise in the shortest duration of time, while at night the signs Cancer to Sagittarius take the longest duration of time.

When the Sun is at summer solstice (zero degrees Sayana Cancer) during the daytime signs Cancer to Sagittarius spend the longest duration of time to rise and during night signs Capricorn to Gemini take the shortest duration of time.

Sign which takes longer time in rising than the time taken by same sign at the equator, is the sign of long ascension and the sign which takes shorter time in rising is the sign of short ascension. **The zodiac signs Capricorn to Gemini are short ascension signs while Cancer to Sagittarius are long ascension signs for northern hemisphere. The opposite holds good for southern hemisphere.** An intuitive way to remember this is that in the northern hemisphere the months from July (Cancer) to December (Sagittarius) see the sun rising a little later when compared to the previous day. As a result, if one were to assume a day as being from one sunrise to another, then the days from July to December would be longer while the days from January through June would be shorter.

As the latitude of the observer increases, the duration of signs of long ascension become much longer while the duration of signs of short ascension become much shorter.

4

Panchangam and Timekeeping

A panchangam or panchanga is a hindu calendar cum almanac that follows the traditional units of Indian timekeeping. Practitioners of vedic astrology rely heavily upon panchangams while making their forecasts and predictions. They also consult the panchāngam to know the auspiciousness of any date and time (muhurtha) for any important undertaking such as a journey, buying and selling a home or vehicle, starting a new job, marriage, puja, festivals, vrata, shraddhas etc. Panchāngams are published in India by many learned authors, academies, and institutions. There are several panchangams that are published on an annual basis. Different publications could see minor time variations given that timekeeping dates back to the vedic age. As a result, we could see astrologers providing different dates for planetary transits. Panchangams forecast celestial phenomena such as the eclipses, forecast weather as well as more mundane occurrences. Panchangams are luni-sidereal in nature.

A typical Panchāngam will provide the positions of the Sun, Moon, and other planets for every day of the year at a fixed location (longitude, latitude) and time of day. Additionally, it will also provide details on lagnas, horas (quality of time based on the day of the week and planetary ruler in undertaking specific tasks), good and bad times in a day etc. The word **ephemeris** is used to describe a manual that gives the position of various astronomical objects for all days of the year at a particular point of time.

The word Panchanga is a sanskrit word which can be divided into 2 parts "panch" and "ang" which literally means having five limbs. The Moon as we have already seen is considered to be the most important planet in vedic astrology and its motions and attributes are considered to be critical in establishing the accuracy of any hindu calendar.

In Vedic astrology the five limbs literally translate into "five attributes" of the day based on the relative motion and position of the Moon and the Sun.

Nakshatra: A nakshatra is a stellar mansion in which Moon is located for an observer at the center of the Earth. One nakshatra equals 13°20'. There are a total of 27 Nakshatras in 360°.

Tithi: A tithi is a lunar day and describes the angular relationship between Sun and Moon. One Tithi equals 12° longitudinal difference between the Moon and the Sun.

Yoga: A Yoga also describes the angular relationship between Sun and Moon(Longitude of Moon + Longitude of Sun). One Yoga equals 13°20'. There are a total of 27 Yogas in 360°.

Karana: A Karana is one-half of a Tithi. One Karana equals 6° longitudinal difference between the Moon and the Sun. There are a total of 11 karanas.

Var / Vaar: One of the seven days of the week (Sunday, Monday, Tuesday, Wednesday, Thursday, Friday, Saturday). The seven classical planets each own 1 day of the week with Sun: Sunday (Ravivaar), Moon: Monday (Somvaar), Mars (Mangalvaar): Tuesday, Mercury: Wednesday (Budhvaar), Jupiter: Thursday (Brihaspativaar), Venus: Friday (Shukravaar) and Saturn: Saturday (Shanivaar).

Certain characteristics associated with people born on different days of the week

Sunday: Those born on this day will talk much, be courageous and like to travel.

Monday: The person born on this day will be soft, calm and truth-loving and have a good personality and strong convictions.

Tuesday: The person born on this day will show anger and courage. They have the capacity to execute their tasks well and also seek favours from women.

Wednesday: The person born on this day will be good to look at and will have high intellectual interests.

Thursday: The person born on this day will be kind, compassionate, practical and eager to use time properly.

Friday: Persons born on this day will prefer white clothes and will be pragmatic.

Saturday: Generally, persons born on this day will be poor, lean and unwise in dealing with others. They will be emotional in nature and may be indiscrete with their emotions.

Hindu Timekeeping

Ancient texts on vedic astrology including the Uttara Kalamrita written by Kalidasa uses the term 'Ghatika' or 'Ghati' to measure the time of the day. Ghatika also goes by the name of 'Nadi'. Each Ghatika consists of 60 'Vighatika' or 'Vighati' or 'Vinadi'.

The day is divided into 60 Ghatikas with each Ghatika consisting of 24 minutes. Thus each Vighatika consists of 24 seconds.

24 Hours = 60 Ghatikas

1 Ghatika = 60 Vighatikas = 24 Minutes

1 Vighatika = 6 Asus = 24 Seconds

Panchangams use Ghatikas for timekeeping.

According to our ancient scriptures, Brahma, the creator, creates and destroys the universe cyclically. The life of Brahma is 120 divine years called Mahakalpa. There are 14 Manus in one divine day called Kalpa of Brahma. The life of each Manu is called Manvantara and it has 71 eras of four quarters. Each quarter has four Yugas – Krita or Satya, Treta, Dvapara and Kali. The following is a list of Vedic units of time and periods.

Truti = Time taken to tear apart the softest petals of a lotus

Krati = 34,000th of a second

100 Trutis = 1 Lub

30 Lub = 1 Nimesh

27 Nimesh = 1 Guru Akshar

10 Guru Akshar = 1 Pran

6 Pran Vighatika = 1 Ghatika

60 Ghatikas = 1 day and night

That means, in a day and night, there are 17,49,60,00,000 trutis Another division of time starts with Tatpara and ends with Kalpa which is 4,320,000,000 sidereal years.

60 Tatparas = 1 Paras

60 Paras = 1 Vilipta

60 Vilipta = 1 Lipta

60 Lipta = 1 Vighatika

60 Vighatika = 1 Ghatika

60 Ghatika = 1 Day

1 Kalpa is known to be equal to 1000 Mahayugs with 4/10ths,

3/10ths, 2/10ths and 1/10th of a Mahayug corresponding to a Satya or Krita Yug, Treta Yuga, Dwapara Yuga and Kali Yuga respectively.

Satya Yug = 4,32,000 * 4 = 17,28,000 years

Treta Yug = 4,32,000 * 3 = 12,96,000 years

Dwapar Yug = 4,32,000 * 2 = 8,64,000 years

Kali Yug = 4,32,000 * 1 = 4,32,000 years

1 Mahayug = 4,320,000 years

71 Mahayug = 30,67,20,000 years = 1 Manvantar

14 Manvantar = 4,29,40,80,000 years

1 Kalpa = 1000 Mahayugs = 4,32,00,00,000 years

Hindu Sunrise

Hindu sunrise and sunset times differ from astronomical sunrise that we see in newspapers.

Astronomical sunrise is defined as time of first appearance of the upper limb or the edge of the disc of the sun on the eastern horizon.

The sunset is the moment of disappearance of the upper limb. For religious and astrological purposes the time when the middle of the sun's disc rises above the eastern horizon is used. All festival determinations are done based on the time when the middle of the disc becomes visible at eastern horizon.

Further, Hindu Sunrise and Sunset ignores refraction which makes the Sun visible even when it is below eastern horizon. Hindu Sunrise is planetary which means that the centre of Earth and Sun should align to eastern horizon.

Hindu Sunrise = Astronomical Sunrise + Time taken by the Sun to rise half of its diameter + Time taken by the Sun to rise further to neutralize refraction effect.

Hindu Sunset = Astronomical Sunset - Time taken by the Sun to set half of its diameter - Time taken by the Sun to set further to neutralize refraction effect.

There is typically a difference of 4 or 5 minutes between Astronomical Sunrise and Hindu Sunrise.

Sidereal Day

As we have already seen in the chapter on Western vs. Vedic Astrology, a Sidereal Day is the time taken by Earth to complete 1 rotation about its axis with reference to any fixed star. It is equal to 23h 56m 4.09s. It is appxoximately 4 minutes less than a solar day by 4 minutes. It also goes by the term nakshatra dina as the duration of 1 nakshatra is on an average equal to a sidereal day.

Savana Day

This also goes by the name of Apparent Solar day. The duration of time of between one sunrise to another sunrise is a Savana Day. A Savana day is less than 24 hours during the period of Uttarayan since the sun rises earlier on each successive day but more than 24 hours during period of Dakshinayan.The Vedic system recognises a day as the duration of time from one sunrise to the next sunrise. This span, known as a Savana day, is measured in units of ghatikas. One Savana day is equal to 60 ghatikas and each ghatika is equal to 60 vighatika.

Solar Day

This is the average length of all days of the year. Its duration is 24 hours.

Local Mean Time

The Local Mean Time or LMT is the noon of local time on any day when the Sun reaches the highest point in the sky. The purpose of a local mean time is to correct the variations in the apparent time (Savana Day) forming a uniform time scale at a specific longitude. This was popular in the 19th century before the introduction of time zones.

LMT can be calculated using the following formula:-

LMT = GMT +- Longitude / 15°

GMT is Greenwich Mean Time and corresponds to 0° longitude. The intuition behind this formula is that there are a total of 360 degrees (180 degrees East and 180 degrees West) and 24 hours (1,440 minutes) in a day, as a result of which every 1° of longitude has a time difference of 4 minutes (1440/360).

Standard Time

This is, of course, the official time followed by each country. India follows the Indian Standard Time or IST which is set to the local mean time of Allahabad (25.15° N and 82.5°E) and is 5 hours and 30 minutes ahead of GMT or Greenwich Mean Time.The Local Mean Time of any place in India can accordingly be adjusted from our LMT / GMT formula.

Equation of Time

The equation of time describes the discrepancy between two kinds of solar time. These are apparent solar time, which directly tracks the motion of the sun, and mean solar time, which tracks a fictitious "mean" sun with noons 24 hours apart. Apparent (or true) solar time can be obtained by measurement of the current position (hour angle) of the Sun, or indicated (with limited accuracy) by a sundial. Mean solar time, for the same place, would be the time indicated by a steady clock set so that over the year its differences from apparent solar time average to zero. The graph of the equation of time is closely approximated by the sum of two sine curves. The curves reflect two astronomical effects, each causing a different non-uniformity in the apparent daily motion of the Sun relative to the stars:

- The obliquity of the ecliptic (the plane of the Earth's annual orbital motion around the Sun), which is inclined by about 23.44 degrees relative to the plane of the Earth's equator; and
- The eccentricity of the Earth's orbit around the Sun, which is about 0.0167.

The equation of time is constant only for a planet with zero axial tilt and zero orbital eccentricity.

Equation of Time = Mean Time – Apparent Time at any moment (Whichever is greater).

Hindu Method of Calculating Sunrise Time

As we have already seen there is a slight variation in the times of the Hindu sunrise and the astronomical sunrise that is reported in the newspapers for any location. Astronomical sunrise takes into account the first appearance of the Sun at the eastern horizon of any location while the Hindu sunrise takes into account the time when the centre of the solar disc rises at the eastern horizon. The two typically vary by about 4-5 minutes.

The Hindu method of calculating the sunrise time at any location is determined by calculating the apparent time of sunrise at that location and adding/subtracting the equation of time to obtain the local mean time of sunrise. Apparent time sunrise calculation assumes noon time as 12 PM and sunrise time as 6 AM for all locations.

The following steps are used in obtaining the mean time of sunrise:-

1. Obtain the Nirayana Longitude of Sun at sunrise for the specified location on the specified date (This information will be available in any Hindu almanac or panchang).
2. Add the Ayanamsa value to obtain the Sayana Longitude of sunrise.
3. Apply the following rule to obtain the difference. The difference can at the most be 90°.- If the sayana longitude of sun < 90°, then difference = sayana longitude at sunrise

- If the sayana longitude of sun is <90° and >180°, then difference = 180° - sayana longitude

- If the sayana longitude of sun is < 180° and > 270°, then difference = sayana longitude - 180°

- If the sayana longitude of sun is <270° and >360°, then difference = 360° - sayana longitude

4. Obtain the first middle and last charakhanda values in Vighatis from table 1 in the appendix for the given location's latitude. The first charakhanda value is the Adi Khanda. The sum of the first and the middle charakhanda is the Madhya khanda while the sum of all 3 charakhandas is anthya khanda.

5. Obtain the first middle and last values from step 4 in Asus (Multiply first middle and last charakhanda values in vighatis by 6 respectively).

6. Divide the difference obtained in step 3 by 30°.

   - If the value in step 6 < 1 then use first charakhanda from step 4 in chara calculation, don't add anything to chara in step 8

   - If the value in step 6 < 2 then use middle charakhanda from step 4 in chara calculation, add Adi khanda to chara in step 8

   - If the value in step 6 < 3 then use last charakhanda from step 4 in chara calculation, add Madhya khanda to chara in step 8

7. Apply the following formula to proportionally obtain chara Chara = (difference / 30°) * charakhanda as per step 6

8. Adjusted Chara = chara + khanda (as per step 6 and 7). This will, of course, be in Vighatis and needs to be converted to Ghatis in step 10.

9. We have seen that a day and night together consist of 60 ghatikas with 1 ghatika (ghati) = 60 vighatika (vighatis). If we make an assumption that the day is 30 ghatis then the time period from sunrise to apparent noon will be 15 ghatis.

10. Dinardha = 15 +- Adjusted Chara (Add if Sun is in Aries through Virgo and Subtract if Sun is in Libra through Pisces). Convert the value obtained in hours and minutes.

11. Apparent Time of Sunrise = 12 Noon – Dinardha

12. Local Mean Time of Sunrise = Apparent Time of Sunrise +- Equation of Time

Example 2:

Calculate the sunrise time for New Delhi, India on 15th August, 2014 AD.

We will first need to obtain the nirayana longitude at sunrise on the day. Any Hindu almanac or panchangam is likely to list the longitude of all the 9 planets either at sunrise time at a location or at 5:30 AM IST for all days of the year with the second being quite common. The Nirayana Longitude at apparent sunrise time of 6 AM on August 15, 2014 at New Delhi = 118°04'. (Please refer chapter on 12 houses of a rasi chart).

Sayana Longitude at Sunrise – Nirayana Longitude + Ayanamsa = 118°4' + 24°3' = 142°7'.

This falls in between 90° and 180°.

Difference = 180° - 142°7' = 37°53'.

New Delhi's latitude is 28°36'north. Let us take the charakhanda values provided in table 1 of Appendix 1 for 28° in vighatis.

Charakhanda 1 = 63.8, Charakhanda 2 = 51.04, Charakhanda 3 = 21.27. Adi Khanda = 63.8, Madhya Khanda = 114.84, Anthya Khanda = 136.1. We now divide the difference obtained by 30°. 37°53' / 30° implies Quotient =1 and Remainder 7°53'.

Thus, we use Charakhanda 2 in the chara calculation.

Chara = (7°53' / 30°) * 51.04 = 13.4221.

Adjusted Chara = Chara + Adi Khanda (As per Step 6)
= 13.4221 + 63.8 = 77.2221 (in vighatis).
Adjusted Chara in Ghatis = 1.287 (77.2221/60).

Dinardha = 15 +- Adjusted Chara (Since this is Tropical Leo we add).

Dinardha = 15 + 1.287 = 16.287 (in ghatis).

Dinardha (in hours) = 16.287 * 0.4 = 6.515.

Apparent Time of Sunrise = 12 PM – Dinardha = 12PM – 6.515 = 5.485.

Apparent Time of Sunrise = 5h29m.

We now have to obtain the Local Mean Time of Sunrise by adjusting the Equation of Time. The Equation of Time value on August 15th is 4 minutes (See Appendix II).

Local Mean Time of Sunrise = 5h29m +4m = 5h33m.

This is, of course, the local mean time of sunrise at New Delhi. The longitude of New Delhi is 77.2° east while that of the Indian Standard Time (IST) is 82.5° east.

If we apply the principle of time difference between local mean time and standard time every 1° longitude corresponds to 4 minutes of time difference. For New Delhi the difference between IST and Local Mean Time is ~21 minutes.

Applying the above principle:-

Hindu Sunrise Time at New Delhi (IST) = ((82.5-77.2)*4) + 5h33m = 5h54m

The above is, of course, the Hindu sunrise time. The astronomical on that day was 5h50m some 4 minutes earlier than the Hindu sunrise.

5

Nakshatras

We often visit a temple and are asked to provide our nakshatras. What exactly is a nakshatra? Nakshatras or Constellations or Asterisms are lunar mansions through which the moon moves in its orbit around the earth. According to the Puranas or classical texts, Daksha the son of Brahma had 89 daughters out of which 27 were married to Chandra or "Moon". These 27 daughters are the nakshatras Ashwini to Revati. Puranas also state that Moon favoured Rohini over thc remaining nakshatras thereby neglecting his responsibilities. As a result, Daksha cursed the Moon to wither and die. The Moon approached and worshipped Lord Shiva, in order to be relieved of this curse. Lord Shiva bestowed Chandra with the boon that he would grow for fifteen days or one half of the month (waxing phase or Shukla Paksha) and keep losing one Kala (Krishna Paksha) and decrease in size for the remaining half of the month.

Table 5: Nakshatra, Gana, Ruling Deilies and Ruling Planets

Number	Nakshatra	Gana	Ruling Deity	Ruling Planet
1	Ashwini	Deva	Twins (Sasra-Satya)	Ketu
2	Bharani	Manushya	Yama	Venus
3	Krittika	Rakshasa	Agni	Sun
4	Rohini	Manushya	Brahma	Moon
5	Mrigashirsha	Deva	Soma	Mars
6	Ardra	Manushya	Rudra	Rahu
7	Punarvasu	Deva	Aditi	Jupiter
8	Pushya	Deva	Brihaspati	Saturn
9	Ashlesha	Rakshasa	Sarpa	Mercury
10	Magha	Rakshasa	Pitr	Ketu
11	Purva Phalguni	Manushya	Bhaga	Venus
12	Uttara Phalguni	Manushya	Aryaman	Sun
13	Hasta	Deva	Savitr	Moon
14	Chitra	Rakshasa	Vishvakarma	Mars

Number	Nakshatra	Gana	Ruling Deity	Ruling Planet
15	Swati	Deva	Vayu	Rahu
16	Vishaka	Rakshasa	Indra + Agni	Jupiter
17	Anuradha	Deva	Mitra	Saturn
18	Jyeshtha	Rakshasa	Indra	Mercury
19	Moola	Rakshasa	Nirrti	Ketu
20	Purva Ashadha	Manushya	Apas	Venus
21	Uttara Ashadha	Manushya	Vishvadeva	Sun
22	Shravana	Deva	Vishnu	Moon
23	Dhanishta	Rakshasa	Vasu	Mars
24	Satabishak	Rakshasa	Varuna	Rahu
25	Purva Bhadrapada	Manushya	Ajaikapada	Jupiter
26	Uttara Bhadrapada	Manushya	Ahirbudhnya	Saturn
27	Revati	Deva	Pushan	Mercury

The 27 nakshatras Ashwini to Revati are further classified as Deva Gana, Manushya Gana and Rakshasa Gana Nakshatras.

Vedic astrology says that people who are born in the Manushya Gana value self-esteem. Natives of this Gana are usually blessed with wealth and they lead an affluent life. People of this Gana have a good physique, tall body structure and big eyes. They possess attractive physique and the well-defined structure of eyes and face enhance their beauty. The people of Manushya Gana have a warm and caring nature. They are very helpful to the distressed people around them.

People born in Dev Gana possess many positive characteristics. They are attractive with a nice physique. Dev Gana makes its native intelligent and sharp. They are simple people with wise thoughts. People of Dev Gana are compassionate and humble; their helping attitude towards the disabled and the poor people is a prominent quality in their nature. They help the distressed people whole-heartedly. The people of Dev Gana do not have voracious appetites and are frugal eaters.

People who have Rakshasa Gana as their birth Gana may have a stubborn and rigid character. They act according to their will which sometimes may not be a good decision. They have a hefty body and may be quite aggressive. They may have a tendency to fight over small issues. These may also sound harsh and may not be able to realize the impact that their words and actions have on the others.

The Gana only indicates the temperament of an individual and, therefore, a person born in a Deva Gana nakshatra need not be good, while a person born in Rakshasa Gana need not be bad.

The 27 nakshatras can be mapped onto one of the 12 Rasis from Mesha to Meena. As mentioned, each of the 12 rasis cover a longitude of 30 degrees with a sum total of 360 degrees. Each Nakshatra lasts on an average for approximately a sidereal day or 23 hours 56 minutes and 4 seconds and covers a longitude of 13°20'. Each Nakshatra is also divided into quarters or 4 padas of 3°20' each.A nakshatra month consists of 27.32 days and nakshatra year consists of 327.84 days.

Table 6: Nakshatra, Pada and Rasi

Number	Nakshatra	Pada – 1	Pada – 2	Pada – 3	Pada - 4	Zodiac
1	Ashwini	Mesha	Mesha	Mesha	Mesha	0° - 13°20' Mesha
2	Bharani	Mesha	Mesha	Mesha	Mesha	13° 20' - 26°40' Mesha
3	Krittika	Mesha	Vrishaba	Vrishaba	Vrishaba	26°40' Mesha - 10° Vrishabha
4	Rohini	Vrishaba	Vrishaba	Vrishaba	Vrishaba	10° - 23°20' Vrishabha
5	Mrigashirsha	Vrishaba	Vrishaba	Mithuna	Mithuna	23° 20' Vrishabha - 6° 40' Mithuna
6	Ardra	Mithuna	Mithuna	Mithuna	Mithuna	6° 40' - 20° Mithuna
7	Punarvasu	Mithuna	Mithuna	Mithuna	Kataka	20° Mithuna - 3°20' Kataka
8	Pushya	Kataka	Kataka	Kataka	Kataka	3°20' - 16°40' Kataka
9	Ashlesha	Kataka	Kataka	Kataka	Kataka	16°40' - 30° Kataka
10	Magha	Simha	Simha	Simha	Simha	0° - 13°20' Simha
11	Purva Phalguni	Simha	Simha	Simha	Simha	13°20' - 26°40' Simha

Number	Nakshatra	Pada – 1	Pada – 2	Pada – 3	Pada - 4	Zodiac
12	Uttara Phalguni	Simha	Kanya	Kanya	Kanya	26°40' Simha-10° Kanya
13	Hasta	Kanya	Kanya	Kanya	Kanya	10° - 23°20' Kanya
14	Chitra	Kanya	Kanya	Tula	Tula	23°20' Kanya - 6°40' Tula
15	Swati	Tula	Tula	Tula	Tula	6°40' - 20° Tula
16	Vishaka	Tula	Tula	Tula	Vrischika	20° Tula - 3°20' Vrischika
17	Anuradha	Vrischika	Vrischika	Vrischika	Vrischika	3°20' - 16°40' Vrischika
18	Jyeshtha	Vrischika	Vrischika	Vrischika	Vrischika	16°40' - 30° Vrischika
19	Moola	Dhanus	Dhanus	Dhanus	Dhanus	0° - 13°20' Dhanus
20	Purva Ashadha	Dhanus	Dhanus	Dhanus	Dhanus	13°20' - 26°40' Dhanus
21	Uttara Ashadha	Dhanus	Makara	Makara	Makara	26°40' Dhanus - 10° Makara
22	Shravana	Makara	Makara	Makara	Makara	10° - 23°20' Makara
23	Dhanishta	Makara	Makara	Kumbha	Kumbha	23°20' Makara - 6°40' Kumbha
24	Satabishak	Kumbha	Kumbha	Kumbha	Kumbha	6°40' - 20° Kumbha
25	Purva Bhadrapada	Kumbha	Kumbha	Kumbha	Meena	20° Kumbha - 3°20' Meena
26	Uttara Bhadrapada	Meena	Meena	Meena	Meena	3°20' - 16°40' Meena
27	Revati	Meena	Meena	Meena	Meena	16°40' - 30° Meena

As can be seen from the table, there are a total of 108 padas (4 padas each for every nakshatra). The 108 padas are subdivided sequentially into 9 padas for each of the 12 rasis. For example, all 4 padas of Ashwini and Bharani nakshatras and the 1st pada of Krittika nakshatra will form part of Mesha rasi. Similarly, the last pada of Punarvasu nakshatra, all 4 padas of Pushya and Ashlesha nakshatras will form part of Kataka rasi. In this sequence of mapping nakshatras onto rasis we can observe the fact that 9 nakshatras will map onto 4 rasis which corroborates the fact the moon takes approximately 2.25 (or 9/4) days to traverse a single zodiac or rasi. All 27 nakshatras also have ruling planet lords in much the same way as the 12 rasis. From the above table we can see the order of the ruling planet lords. Ashwini is ruled by Ketu while Ashlesha is ruled by Mercury; Uttara Phalguna is ruled by Sun while Anuradha is ruled by Saturn. It is also observed that the ruling planetary lords follow an order from Ketu to Mercury and if the difference between 2 nakshatras is equal to 9, then the pair will be ruled by the same planet (eg: Ardra (No.6) and Swati (No.15) are both ruled by Rahu).

In addition to the 27 nakshatras there is a 28th named Abhijit (meaning victorious) which is seldom used as a nakshatra. It appears between Uttara Ashadha and Shravana. Its longitude runs from the last quarter of Uttara Ashādhā to first part of Shravana. Abhijit nakshatra is not a regular nakshatra with four padas or quarters, it serves as an intercalary asterism most of the times.Abhijit is a male nakshatra unlike the remaining 27 nakshatras which are feminine in naturc. Its ruling deity is said to be Lord Brahma or the creator himself. It is said that 24 minutes before and 24 minutes after midnight as well as 24 minutes before and 24 minutes after midday is called Abhijit Muhurtha. This Muhurtha is said to completely destroy evil propensities of unknown bodies including stars and planets. Both Lord Rama and Lord Krishna were said to be born during this time period.The presence of a 28th asterism is consistent with the fact that Moon takes 27.32 days to make a complete revolution around Earth.

Fun Math:

We are now cognizant of the fact a nakshatra month lasts for 27.32 days. Given that there are 365 days in a solar year we can confidently state that all 27 nakshatras will occur at least 13 times in a solar year (27.32 * 13 =

355.16 days) and ~10 nakshatras will occur a 14th time in that same solar year. We can also see that if a nakshatra were to occur on a particular day of a year, on the same day the following year will see the moon transiting the 10th nakshatra from the 1st nakshatra seen the previous year. For example, if July 20th, 2014 happens to be Bharani nakshatra then July 20th 2015 is likely to see the Moon traversing the Purva Phalguni nakshatra. It is also common to see that the Moon is Trine its position the previous year. In this example, Moon is in Aries in July 2014 while it is in Leo in July 2015.

Following is the list of 27 nakshatras and certain characteristics associated with them:-

Ashwini

A person born in this Nakshatra is inclined towards serving others, is humble by nature, is truthful, has a contented family life. Ashwini Nakshatra brings about quick aid and energization. People born in Ashwini are very active, always busy doing something and they will spend their time keeping their house neat and clean. Ashwini rules all forms of transportation and fast travel.This represents a person with a happy, carefree disposition, very intelligent. Vast learning, well developed brain power, faith in religion, sacrificing tendency, ambitions, philosophical and social are the traits of those born under this nakshatra. It is ruled by Ketu.

Bharani

Bharani, means "The Bearing Star", also known as "The Star of Restraint". The planet of art and beauty, the Venus, rules this nakshatra. Bharani Nakshatra takes away that which has reached its term of life to a new condition. It shows the movement of the soul away from the body. It conveys ideas pertaining to discipline, self-control to be faithful, be firm, enduring supporting, maintaining, nourishing etc. In case of strong malefic influences , persons may develop extreme tendencies like crimes, murders, terrorism, etc. If a person is born in this Nakshatra, he is cruel, ungrateful and no sense of indebtness, achieves notoriety, fears water, is restless and wicked; but is also stable, knowledgeable, frank and truthful. An interesting feature of those born in Bharani is that they are quiet fond of spreading rumors. They act more like a leader of a group, rather than an ordinary family member. Bharani-born have a magnetic personality, changing moods are business minded, influential and occupy a high position.

Krittika

Kritikka is considered the nakshatra where power is born. It is ruled by Sun. The passivity of this nakshatra represents its ability to nurture power. Krittika suggests passivity, indicating that Krittika needs outer energy or a life circumstance to activate its power. Krittika Nakshatra burns up negativity, purifies what is mixed, and cooks or prepares that which is not yet ripe.This nakshatra rules war, battles, and disputes. People with this nakshatra have a cutting wit and can be sarcastic and critical. They are stubborn, aggressive and can be very angry. Those born under Krittika nakshatra have strained relations with relatives and friends. However, these persons are gluttons, fond of spicy foods, well-versed academically, fond of opposite sex, bright in appearance, misers, of a worried nature and of widespread fame. Those born on a Krittika day are fiery and full of creative energy. They like to take on big projects and are highly ambitious and self-motivated.Vast learning, logical, doubting mind, creative ability, unsteady fortune, enthusiastic, engineering brain and bravery are their typical characteristics.

Rohini

As described earlier of the 27 daughters of Daksha, Rohini is considered to be Moon's favorite wife. This is the fourth nakshatra of the zodiac, ruled by the planet Moon. Eyes of the people born in this nakshatra are especially attractive. 'Rohini' is the wife of Chandra who is said to have been fond of fine dress, cosmetics and décor and was the most beloved of Chandra or Moon. Those born in the star Rohini are agriculturists, experts, well-behaved, handsome, good speakers and poets. Rohini Nakshatra evokes some degree of jealousy, because others may resent that a person gains such abundance. It can increase desire. But these are only side effects to its great prosperity. A person born in this Nakshatra is efficient in religious activities, is endowed with beauty, is a master-conversationalist, a genius and efficient in arts. They are extremely materialistic and frown on those who don't measure up to their taste and high culture. One who is born under this star will have to control his/

her stubborn nature if they want to work in groups or be in professions that require dealing with people. They are also short tempered and invite troubles. They possess inherent aptitude for any work entrusted to them. They can attain great success in their life, provided a little restraint is kept in the freedom of his mind. Those born under this nakshatra are well learned, influential, travel minded, artistic, business like, spiritual and of changing affections. It is the birth star of Lord Krishna.

Mrigashirsha

The word 'Mriga' represents forests, gardens, a search, a seeking to find, to roam about in forests and a hunter, to seek to blaze the trail, a guide and preceptor. Mrigashirsha is partly in Vrishabha and partly in Mithuna.It conveys the ideas of searching for beautiful faces, visit or request a girl in marriage. People born in this nakshatra have a strong body and moderate complexion.They are sincere in their behavior towards others and expect that others should also behave in the same way, in reciprocation. They have a good grasping power, can quickly learn new things and have a creative nature.A person born in this Nakshatra is a sharp shooter, loved by the king and follows virtuous path.They always have financial and personal difficulties. Vast learning, likes research, high position, noble views of life, mystical are some of the traits exhibited by those born under Mrigashirsa nakshatra. It is ruled by Mars.

Ardra

Those born in the Ardra star are soft, stable minded, strong, earning by sacrifice, afflicted by sickness, fear and angry. Ardra born people can behave very coolly during the times of extreme hardship and plan their actions accordingly; and they get employed in professions that are related with travel and foreign places. One born under this nakshatra is thrifty, insincere, ungrateful and sinful and, at times, they will spend foolishly. They are flexible and open to change, and often make attempts to change their negative traits. Those born under this nakshatra will suffer from heart trouble, paralysis, and stress related ailments.They are religious, of responsible disposition, artistic, brave, prone to litigations, have laziness, have leadership qualities and passionate. It is ruled by Rahu.

Punarvasu

Punarvasu Nakshatra brings about the return of energy and vitality. It causes our creative growths and inspirations to be renewed. It denotes the ideas of abode, residence, back to home, sojourn, recurrence, commencement, to shine or grow bright again, to enter into life again, renewal of riches etc. A person born in this Nakshatra has numerous friends, is a practitioner of sacred texts and scriptures, possesses gems, jewels and ornaments etc. and has the spirit to rise from the ashes. These people have a good height and an oval face. They tend to be obese in their later age. People born in this nakshatra can shine and get success in almost all the subjects, except in partnership businesses or deals. They do not like to cause trouble to others; on the other hand, they try to help the needy.Those born in this nakshatra are good natured, have trials in life, are cultured, helping nature, vanity minded, failure and success come often.It is ruled by Jupiter. It is the birth star of Lord Rama.

Pushya

The word Pushya means to strengthen, to fortify. The word etymologically means "to nourish" and that again means to preserve, to protect, replenish, multiply and strengthen. Pushya Nakshatra increases our good karma and good efforts. The value of this Nakshatra for religious and spiritual practices is emphasized. The person born under this Nakshatra has a healthy body, obeys his parents, religious, humble, fortunate and possesses wealth and vehicles etc.These people respect laws and believe that nobody should be above the law. These people are likely to suffer from lack of hormones that help in body growth and digestion, skin troubles, cough and cold and asthma. They are devotional, wealthy, doubting, soft nature, jack of all trades and well placed. Pushya is ruled by Saturn.

Ashlesha

Ashlesha Nakshatra can be helpful if we have enemies but it can serve to give a person an inimical temperament as well. It all depends upon how the energy of this Nakshatra is used. A person born in 'Ashlesha Nakshatra' is a born wanderer i.e. travels unnecessarily, wicked, causes anguish to others, spends his wealth for evil purposes, and is a sensualist. Their disease resistant capacity (immunity) is limited. They tend to put on weight in the middle age. They are actively associated with organisation or persons or services where some underhand dealings are undertaken.

They also make successful politicians. These people can make some of the best statesmen, given a favourable combination of planets like Jupiter, Sun and Mars.They have excellent communication skills and many of them are good orators. They make for good administrators. Those born in the Nakshatra of Ashlesha are moody, short tempered , have harsh speech, wealthy, religious and slow in their deeds. Mercury rules this nakshatra.

Magha

Magha stands for noble impulses and incentives, the gift of Magha must always be a noble one. It shows that we are coming to the end of a cycle. Its condition is prior to that of Bharani which indicates the movement of the soul away from the body. A person born in this Nakshatra is strong-hearted, respects his father, is a learned man, intelligent and is a winner. Magha born will respect the elders and gain from their experience. They are straight forward, do not like to harm others and expect that others, too, should not harm them in any way. These people are often failures if they undertake independent business, as reckless profit making is not in their blood. A person born in this Nakshatra will respect others and reciprocally, expect respect from them. Those born under this nakshatra could suffer from diseases like asthma, epilepsy or cancer. They have the capacity to command, are wealthy, devoted, social workers and have moral standard. Magha is ruled by Ketu.

Purva Phalguni

Purva Phalguni brings about union and procreation on all levels. This nakshatra implies by the bed or hammock, it is a time of rest and relaxation. Purva Phalguni is the symbol of good fortune and luck. A person born in this Nakshatra is very brave, fosters many people, clever but cunning, lusty and rough.They will have a long face and are generally handsome. They do not like underhand dealings and given a chance, would like to prevent others from indulging in those activities. Their independent nature often makes them difficult to enjoy the confidence of their superiors. These people eat a lot and tend to suffer from headache, sinus or high blood pressure. A person born in this Nakshatra tends to be scrupulously honest and cannot stand back quietly and watch any illegal activity. Those born under this nakshatra could suffer from ailments like asthma and related breathing troubles, dental problems and abdominal complications. Purva Phalguni is ruled by Venus.

Uttara Phalguni

Uttara Phalguni indicates both the need for union and for organizing the resources gained through it. A person born in this nakshatra is charitable, kind hearted, possesses patience and achieves fame.They are straight forward and do not like to be taken for granted by others.Those born under this nakshatra have a strong physique, good eyesight and are generally very ambitious. The efforts undertaken by these people have a certain aura of royal authority around them. They will enjoy a satisfactory married life and they are happy with their family. Uttara Phalguni particularly has special reference to patronage, favour, granting reliefs, person approached for monetary help or relief in sickness. A person born in this nakshatra will especially be successful in careers that are associated with new beginnings like construction industry, hospitality industry, event planning, publicity management etc.Those born under this nakshatra could suffer from ailments like dental problems, gastric problems and bodily discomforts. Uttara Phalguni is ruled by Sun.

Hasta

Hasta gives the ability to achieve our goals in a complete and immediate manner. A person born in this nakshatra is famous, religious minded, respects Brahmins and learned people and possesses wealth.They are tall and thin in physical appearance.They know how to win over the other party, hence these people can be good diplomats or are suitable for any profession. They do not have the formal education, but they can carry out the responsibilities assigned to them through their all round knowledge and efforts. A person born in this nakshatra is a very creative person and work very well with his/her hands. Again, those who are born under this nakshatra are good at organizing and managing things.They also excel at jobs, which involve a lot of travelling. People born in Hasta tend to suffer from cough, cold and asthma. It is ruled by Moon.

Chitra:

Chitra allows us to gain the fruit of our good karma that comes through righteousness. It has a highly spiritual energy and effect. A person born in this Nakshatra defeats his enemies gallantly, is an expert in politics and has extraordinary intelligence.They enjoy good health and always appear much younger than their actual age. Many of them will pursue higher education and will retain a lifelong thirst for knowledge. Those born under this nakshatra could suffer from ailments like kidney and bladder troubles, psychiatric and brain disorders etc. They are learned, sickly, magicians, superstitious, tactful and of hard mind. The fiery Mars rules this nakshatra.

Swati

A person born in this Nakshatra is endowed with tremendous beauty, flirts with many women, is jolly and receives wealth from the king. They neither like to do any injustice to others, nor do they like any injustice being done to them. Swati people have an ability to "bend with the wind" in order to survive the forces of change which they may encounter. A person born under this star is good at buying and selling, his wealth and property come and go quite easily. They are broad-minded and attract people from diverse backgrounds. Many of those born under this nakshatra will be involved in religious or social work. Swati's primary motivation is artha or material prosperity. Rahu, the ruling planet, can create a strong desire for financial success and lust for life. They are cultured, learned, famous, submissive to ladies, passionate and wealthy.

Vishaka

A person born in this nakshatra is religious minded having inclination towards performing rites and rituals etc., is of unstable nature and unfriendly. Vishaka born have a well-proportioned body, but they tend to be obese and put on weight with the passing of age. Vishaka people can be envious or covetous of the success of others. They may lack a strong social network of friends and feel isolated and alone against the world. Bitterness and resentment may result. Those born under this nakshatra are likely to have a very happy marital life and will make good marriage partners. They are excellent communicators, and they write and speak well. They need to have a well balanced diet and should exercise regularly to keep them fit.They will have a sweet tongue and quiet diplomatic in their choice of words.They are dreamers, administrators, brave, strong and of charitable nature. Jupiter rules Vishaka.

Anuradha

Anuradha Nakshatra gives balance in relationship, both honouring others and seeking ourselves to be honourable. A person born in this Nakshatra possesses lustre and splendour, achieves fame, is enthusiastic, a destroyer of his enemies, an expert in many forms of arts and a sensualist. They can reside in foreign lands and achieve success away from their homeland. Anuradha people usually possess good health and vitality. Called the "star of success," Anuradha natives can demonstrate organizational skills and call others to activity and development. Some of them may be creative, especially in the performing arts. Many of them will shine in social and political fields. Those born under this nakshatra could suffer from minor bodily ailments like asthma, breathing trouble, cough and cold and dental problems. They need to watch their dietaryhabits due to an inability to bear hunger or thirst. They have a strong appetite for life in general. They are learned, have deep devotion, softness, musical talents, royal position, quickness. Saturn is the planetary ruler.

Jyeshtha

Jyestha means the eldest one, the senior most, the chief one, more excellent than, preferred one or someone or something supreme glorious. The person born under this star is full of lustre and splendour, achieves fame and greatness, is rich, brave, a hero and an excellent conversationalist. Jyeshta allows us to reach the summit of our personal powers but it requires great courage and effort. People born in this nakshatra possess a mix of the qualities of Mercury and Mars. Jyeshta born have excellent physical stamina and a handsome physical appearance.The qualities make them appear like a very proud person, but the facts are actually different. The people born under this star are not very clear about the profession they want to pursue for life, and could keep on changing jobs or the lines of business often. They are an expert at working with their hands and at fashioning metals.They can be involved in religious practices while, simultancously, entrenched in materialistic pursuits. The primary motivation of Jyeshta is artha or material prosperity. They are artistic, lover of ornaments and costly dresses, dreamers, brave, agriculturists, philosophical and well-talented. Mercury rules this asterism.

Moola

Moola signifies roots, that is to say, everything of basic nature, its motion is finite and limited. Moola connotes the ideas of foundation, commencement, from the very bottom, the chief or principal city or the capital. Moola does not indicate fortune or luck. The people born on this nakshatra will be financially successful and lead a materially comfortable life. The ruler of this lunar mansion is Ketu, the South Node of the Moon. The Moola individual may possess a deep philosophical nature and an inquisitive mind that enjoys exploring the roots of any subject. The people born in this nakshatra gain the wisdom and knowledge through their hard work. They cause destruction to their families. They are peace loving personalities, but will not hesitate to fight for what rightfully belongs to them. Moola born people have multiple skills and, hence, change of professions is a regular feature for these people and they spend their money recklessly. They are ambitious, learned, wavering, writers, proud, talkative, travellers and very helpful.

Purva Ashadha

People born in Purva Ashadha are intelligent and convincing. Purva Ashadha means the undefeated or unsubdued and is called the invincible star. Its natives are very proud people with the ability to influence and empathize with the masses. Purva Ashadha usually brings fame, wealth, fertility and much wisdom. They tend to get into arguments with others, sort out the contentions issues, and prove their intelligence through the arguments.They lack the necessary logical reasoning to take a well thought out decision. These natives can exhibit an over-expansive nature, and usually do what they like without considering others opinions. They are good debaters and can defeat anyone in an argument. They can become obstinate and will not submit to the demands of anyone. Purva Ashadha born seriously start thinking about pursuing any of their interests. They are clever, helpful, brave, conspirers, selfish, evil minded and wealthy. Venus is the ruling lord.

Uttara Ashadha

Uttara Ashadha born can be driven like a workaholic, extremely persistent when excited, but if they lose interest they become lazy, introspective, and not finish what they started. A strongly placed moon in the natal chart of some Uttara Ashadha born can give them a fair complexion. The people born under this nakshatra do not trust others easily and it is only after spending considerable time with them that others can get an entry into the inner circle of their friends. Good Mercury placed in their natal chart could make them a good consultant or advisor in any field. They are usually preachers, respected, noble, basting, of wavering mind and often short tempered. Sun rules this nakshatra.

Shravana

Shravana usually means "hearing". The symbol of Shravana is three footprints. It is the birth star of Saraswati.Shravana enables to link people together by connecting them to their appropriate paths in life. A person born in this Nakshatra is well versed in the sacred texts and scriptures, has many sons and friends, and destroys his enemies. These people like to mingle with others and have a large network of friends. Shravana born people are ready to help others, they seldom gain the respect and faith of those whom they help. Those who are born under this nakshatra will be financially successful and lead a materially comfortable life. Those born under this nakshatra could suffer from ailments like eczema and skin diseases, T.B., rheumatism etc. They are brave, administrators, adaptable, tactful, wealthy, have evil company and are slow in their deeds. Moon rules this nakshatra.

Dhanishta

A person born in this nakshatra is of excellent behaviour, practical, rich, powerful and kind hearted. People born in this nakshatra are lean and tall, with good ability to resist contagious diseases. These people get angry and are determined to crush the offender with all their might. These people need to take proper care of their health, as they tend to neglect their health problems till they reach the extreme stage. Dhanishta born are passionate about the past and spend time in learning about it. Dhanishta Nakshatra has one uncommon characteristic denoting delayed marriage or unhappy married life. Those born under this nakshatra could suffer from complaints like anaemia, cough and cold etc. They are patient, suffering, royal life, enduring, revengeful, brave and social. Mars rules this nakshatra.

Satabishak

Satabishak brings about a healing crisis leading to revitalization. A person born in this Nakshatra is brave, clever and destroys his enemies. People born in this nakshatra are very simple, principled people living a simple, straightforward life. Satabishak born are ideally suited for any scientific career or a research job. Satabishak born are very changeable and often confuse people. Those born under this nakshatra could suffer from complaints like urinary tract diseases, diabetes, breathing trouble, cough and cold, pneumonia etc. They are cultured, artistic, writers, sacrificing, submissive to the fairer sex, soft hearted and religious. The illusionary Rahu rules this asterism.

Purva Bhadrapada

Purva Bhadrapada raises up our spiritual aspiration in life and takes us out of the domain of selfish behavior. This is a transformational nakshatra where they will sacrifice themselves for a higher cause, to make a difference in the world. A person born in this Nakshatra has full control over his sense organs, is intelligent, an expert in all art forms, and destroys his enemies. Purva Bhadrapada born are risk takers and their charming personality often gets them out of tight spots. A person born in the first three quarters of this nakshatra has a slender, tall stature. Purva Bhadrapada born have a set of principles in their life, which they like to follow under any circumstances. Purva Bhadrapada born are a very adaptable kind and can change themselves as the situation warrants. They spend money in the most appropriate way, avoiding any misuse of the same. Purva Bhadrapada born are engaged in the revenue collection department or in any capacity where cash transactions take place. They are a little more practical minded when it comes to charity. Those born under this nakshatra could suffer from complaints like paralytic attacks, diabetes, gastric and abdominal problems. They are spiritual, unattached, helpful, unknown, patient, boasting, quarrelsome and famous. Jupiter rules this nakshatra.

Uttara Bhadrapada

Uttara Bhadrapada is known as the "Warrior Star". Uttara Bhadrapada grants growth and prosperity in a broad way, benefiting the entire world. A person born in this nakshatra is rich and famous and follows the virtuous path. These people are the real believers in the power of knowledge. Uttara Bhadrapada born are loving and merciful people and always willing to reach out to others.They tend to make a fortune at a place far away from their place of birth. Marital life will be harmonious and satisfactory and children will be a source of joy and happiness.Their behavior is extremely cordial, respectful and praise worthy. They will not hesitate to sacrifice even their own lives for the sake of those who love them. One who is born under this nakshatra could suffer from minor complaints like bodily aches and pains, rheumatism etc. They are soft, helpful, suspicious, learned, devotional, religious, planning. Saturn rules this nakshatra.

Revati

A person born in this nakshatra has amicable nature, controls his senses, acquires wealth by just means and possesses sharp intelligence. A person born in the Revati nakshatra is short tempered and it is very difficult to make them accept the view, which does not suit their principles in life. Revati born persons are the most God fearing and religiously much inclined. These people have to depend on their own efforts to make progress in life. Revati born will have a tendency to overburden themselves with others' problems and this could cause their health to suffer. Marital life will be very harmonious and their spouses are very compatible. They are also good at jobs that require repetitive skills.They may be an Ambassador or a person representing their country for cultural or political matters. They will be interested in the scientific solutions, historical research and ancient cultures. Those born under this nakshatra could suffer from complaints like ulcers, intestinal disorders, orthopaedic and dental problems. They are artistic, have divine qualities, are noble, successful and well-respected in society. Mercury is the planetary ruler of this nakshatra.

6

Tithis

The Moon as we know traverses across 27 nakshatras or asterisms in approximately a sidereal day.The time, which the Moon requires to travel over the 27th part of the ecliptic, is termed as a nakshatra. These nakshatras reflect the number of days in a sidereal month (27.32 days). A Tithi, on the other hand is a lunar day or the time it takes for the longitudinal angle between the sun and the moon to increase by 12°. They last for a duration of anywhere between 19 and 26 hours.

There are 2 lunar phases in vedic astrology as the Moon orbits around Earth, **Shukla Paksha** (Waxing Moon) and **Krishna Paksha** (Waning Moon). Ancient texts talk about Chandra or the moon god approaching Lord Shiva to be relieved of a curse which resulted in the formation of the 2 pakshas. A 'Paksha' literally means a side. Shukla means 'White' or 'Bright' while Krishna means 'Dark' or 'Black'.

A lunar month or synodic month of Moon typically lasts for 29 days 12 hours and 44 minutes or 29.53 days and is divided equally into the two aforementioned pakshas. A lunar year thus consists of 29.53 * 12 or 354.36 days.

Shukla Paksha lasts for one-half of a lunar month or a fortnight and is the period between the new moon day (Amavasya) and full moon day (Poornima). Krishna Paksha also lasts for a fortnight and is the period between the full moon day and new moon day.

The New Moon or Amavasya day which recurs approximately every 30 days and lasts for duration of 19 to 26 hours is the time period when the Moon lies closest to the Sun in the sky as seen from the Earth. It is the instant when the Moon and the Sunare in conjunction as seen from the earth and have the same ecliptical longitude. The Moon is not visible on such days. Solar Eclipses or Surya Grahanam occur on a New Moon Day. On such a day the Sun and the Moon are not only in conjunction with each other but also conjunct one of the 2 lunar nodes (Rahu or Ketu).

The Full Moon or Poornima Day which also recurs once a month is the day when the moon is in opposition to the sun (when it is in the opposite side of the earth from the sun) and the ecliptic longitudes of the sun and the moon differ by 180 degrees. The Moon is completely illuminated as seen from the earth. Lunar Eclipses or Chandra Grahanam occur on Full Moon Day. On such a day the Sun is conjunct with one of the 2 lunar nodes while Moon is in conjunction with the other lunar node.

Following is the list of Tithis and certain characteristics associated with them:-

Table 7: Tithi and Ruling Deity

Number	Tithi	Ruling Deity
1	Prathama (Pratipada)	Agni
2	Dwitiya	Brahma
3	Tritiya	Gauri
4	Chaturthi	Yama / Ganapati
5	Panchami	Naaga
6	Shashti	Kartikeya
7	Saptami	Surya
8	Ashtami	Rudra (Shiva)
9	Navami	Devi Ambika
10	Dasami	Dharmaraja
11	Ekadasi	Rudra (Shiva)
12	Dwadasi	Vishnu / Aditya
13	Trayodasi	Kamadev
14	Chaturdasi	Kali
15	Poornima (Full Moon)	Moon
16	Amavasya (New Moon)	Pitru - Devas

According to Mansagari (A popular classical treatise on Hindu predictive astrology), those born during Shukla Paksha have the capability to develop their potential to the fullest and rise in life through their own effort. Mansagari states that "A person born in Shukla Paksha is elegant like full Moon, wealthy, industrious, well read in shastras, efficient and learned". It also goes on to say that an individual born in Krishna Paksha is : "cruel, harsh in speech, hates women, dull-witted, earns livelihood with the help of others and has a big family." Another classical text on Indian Astrology Yavana Jataka provides brief descriptions on certain qualities of natives born under specific tithis.

Prathama (Pratipada): The presiding deity of the first lunar day is Agni and it is good for all types of auspicious and religious ceremonies. A person born on this day will have a good wife and also enjoy extra-marital relationships.

Dwitiya: Bramha rules this lunar day which is good for the laying of foundations for buildings and other things of a permanent nature. A person born on this day will seek the truth. Such an individual will be liked by all and will be skilled in using weapons.

Tritiya: Gauri is the lord of this day and is good for the cuttings of one's hair and nails and shaving. A person born on this day will be immoral, will be after immoral women and will also be bent on harming others.

Chaturthi: Yama/Ganapati are the lords of the 4th lunar day, which is good for the destruction of one's enemies, the removal of obstacles, and acts of combat. A person born on this day will be greedy, unhelpful to others and secretive.

Panchami: The Naaga or Serpents rule this day, which is favourable for administering medicines, purging of poisons and surgery. A person born on this day will be intelligent long lived and will possess a strong moral character.

Shashti: Kartikeya presides over this day which is favourable for coronations, meeting new friends, festivities, and enjoyment. A person born on this day will have more male issues, will be after sensual pleasures and will have a big circle of friends.

Saptami: The 7th lunar day is ruled by Surya; one may begin a journey, buy conveyances, and deal with other such things as a movable nature. A person born on this day will be rich, will have good character. He/She will respect elders and learned men.

Ashtami: Rudra rules this day, which is good for taking up arms, building of one's defenses, and fortification. A person born on this day will be faithful to the spouse, shall have many interests and speak well.

Navami: Ambika rules this day, which is suitable for killing enemies, acts of destruction, and violence. A person born on this day will be passionate and courageous. He/She will be interested in arts and will be deadly to his/her opponents.

Dasami: This day is ruled by Dharmaraja and is auspicious for acts of virtue, religious functions, spiritual practices, and other pious activities. A person born on this day will be highly successful in business pursuits and will also be well-versed in the sciences.

Ekadasi: Rudra rules this day; fasting, devotional activities, and remembrance of the Supreme Lord are very favourable. A person born on this day will be unprincipled, jealous of other's progress. Such an individual's mind will be occupied by thoughts of women.

Dwadasi: The Vishnu or Aditya rules this day, which is auspicious for religious ceremonies the lighting of the sacred fire, and the performance of one's duties. A person born on this day will be popular with women and amass wealth. This person will have many enemies.

Trayodasi: This day is ruled by Kamadev and is good for forming friendships, sensual pleasures, and festivities. A person born on this day will have a wide circle of relatives and will make them happy. Such an individual will be pure at heart and enjoys good health.

Chaturdasi: Kali rules this day which is suitable for administering poison and calling of elementals and spirits. A person born on this day will have a healthy body and a great personality and will also have convictions of his/her own on everything.

Amavasya: The Pitru-devas rule the New Moon suitable for the propitiation of the Manes and performance of austerities. A person born on this day will become deadly to his/her opponents and will enjoy a good life.

Poornima: Purnima is ruled by Moon and suitable for merry making,fire sacrifice. A person born on this day will keep long hair, live up to 80 years of age and will be efficient in all undertakings.

A Tithi is calculated using the following formula

Tithi(DOY) = Longitude of Moon – Longitude of Sun (of the orbit of 360°)

One *Tithi* ends at the moment of time when the angular distance between the Sun and the Moon becomes an integral multiple of 12°.

1 Tithi = Longitude difference of 12° between the Moon and the Sun.

Table 8: Tithi and Longitudes

Number	Longitude Difference*	Shukla Paksha Tithi	Number	Longitude Difference	Krishna Paksha Tithi
1	0 - 12°	Prathama	16	180 - 192°	Prathama
2	12 - 24°	Dwitiya	17	192 - 204°	Dwitiya
3	24 - 36°	Tritiya	18	204 - 216°	Tritiya
4	36 - 48°	Chaturthi	19	216 - 228°	Chaturthi
5	48 - 60°	Panchami	20	228 - 240°	Panchami
6	60 - 72°	Shashti	21	240 - 252°	Shashti
7	72 - 84°	Saptami	22	252 - 264°	Saptami
8	84 - 96°	Ashtami	23	264 - 276°	Ashtami
9	96 - 108°	Navami	24	276 - 288°	Navami
10	108 - 120°	Dasami	25	288 - 300°	Dasami
11	120 - 132°	Ekadasi	26	300 - 312°	Ekadasi
12	132 - 144°	Dwadasi	27	312 - 324°	Dwadasi
13	144 - 156°	Trayodasi	28	324 - 336°	Trayodasi
14	156 - 168°	Chaturdasi	29	336 - 348°	Chaturdasi
15	168 - 180°	Poornima	30 (0)	348 - 360°	Amavasya

**Indicates difference in longitude between the Moon and the Sun.*

Fun Math: The above table works as a guide in predicting anyone among the sidereal month (sun sign), rasi + nakshatra (moon sign), and tithi provided we know two of them in advance.

Example 3:

If the Sun's longitude is say 130 degrees and the Moon's longitude is 186 degrees this would translate into a longitudinal difference of 56 degrees. We can see from the table that this translates into Shukla Paksha Panchami Tithi.From table 2 we can see that the Sun's Longitude of 130 degrees falls under the 5th month of the vedic calendar or Simha Masa (Leo). Moon's Longitude of 186 degrees falls under Tula rasi Chitra nakshatras (see table 6).

Example 4:

Let us assume the lunar day happens to be Krishna Paksha Ekadasi and the nakshatra happens to be Revati which happens to fall under Meena rasi. Moon's longitude will fall under the range of 346°40'- 360°. Applying our formula of Longitude of Sun = Longitude of Moon – Tithi we will obtain Longitude of Sun = 34°40' - 60°. This range falls under 2nd month of vedic calendar or Vrishaba masa (Taurus).

It can be observed that specific nakshatras fall on specific tithis during specific months. For example the asterism of Pushya will invariably fall on the full moon day or Poornima (subject to longitudinal difference) during makara masa or month of Capricorn according to sidereal astrology.

The Hindu festival of Diwali or Deepavali which falls on New Moon Day as per the Gregorian calendar will fall between mid October and mid November. Per the Sidereal Zodiac the Sun would be in Tula. Given that the New Moon day is the day when Sun and Moon are conjunct the Moon sign would also be Tula Rasi. Diwali day falls under one of the 3 tula rasi nakshatras Chitra, Swati or Vishaka.

Mathematically speaking

If *Longitude of Moon – Longitude of Sun> 0*

{

Longitude of Moon – Longitude of Sun <180°

Tithi Phase = Shukla Paksha

Else

Tithi Phase = Krishna Paksha

}

If *Longitude of Moon – Longitude of Sun< 0*

{

Longitude of Moon – Longitude of Sun >180°

Tithi Phase = Shukla Paksha

Else

Tithi Phase = Krishna Paksha

}

In a rasi chart when the Moon is placed in the 1st seven houses from the Sun (clockwise) this would mean that the tithi is a shukla paksha tithi else it is a krishna paksha tithi. One must however check the longitudinal positions of these 2 planets before arriving at an answer.

7

Yogas

A yoga or a birth yoga is the ending moment of the angular relationship between Sun and Moon. It is one of the attributes of a day that a panchang lists and is one of the limbs of the panchang.There are a total of 27 birth yogas which follows from the fact that 1 yoga equals 13°20' and 360° / 13°20' = 27 yogas in 360 degrees. Practitioners of Astrology also use the terms Nitya Yoga or Dina Yoga when describing birth yogas. The duration of any birth yoga could vary but typically its duration is equal to a sidereal day.

There are a few methods used for calculating the birth yogas of an individual. One such approach uses the following method.

Birth Yoga = Longitude of Sun + Longitude of Moon (Based on the birth/rasi chart of the individual) (If the longitude of sum of Sun and Moon is more than 360 degrees, we subtract 360 from the result to arrive at the birth yoga)

The maximum possible sum of the longitude of the Sun and Moon is 360 + 360 = 720°.

A yoga like a tithi is a pointer to the proximity of the Sun and the Moon and is connected to the 27 nakshatras. According to history, Moon is known to have 16 kalas (Amrita, Manada, Poosha, Tusthi, Pusthi, Rati, Dhruti, Sasichini, Chandrika, Kanta, Jyostna, Shree, Preeti, Angada, Poorna and Poornamruta) or phases (Prathama to Chaturdasi + Amavasya + Poornima). Out of these 16 kalas one is not visible. These 16 kalas are ruled by 16 nitya devis (Maha Tripura Sundari, Kameswari, Bhagamalini, Nityaklinna, Bherunda, Vanhivasini, Maha Vajreswari, Shivadooti (Roudri), Twarita, Kulasundari, Nitya, Neelapataka, Vijaya, Sarvamangala, Jwalamalini and Chidroopa (Chitra)), out of which Maha Tripura Sundari or Devi Para Shakti is not visible to normal mortals. On the day of Full Moon or Poornima all 15 nitya devis are in the Moon, as a result of which the Moon shines brightly. On the following day (Krishna Paksha Prathama) 1 nitya leaves the Moon and as a consequence, the Moon's size gets reduced marginally. This pattern recurs for 15 days till all 15 nityas leave the Moon and the Moon becomes invisible in the sky. This is, of course, the New Moon or Amavasya day. The following day 1 nitya returns to the Moon and Moon starts becoming visible slowly. This pattern is, of course, repeated till the 15th day which is the Full Moon Day. One Shukla Paksha and one Krishna Paksha together constitutes a ~30 day lunar month. 12 such months form a ~360 day lunar year. As the nityas move in and out of the Moon during the 30 day period there are a total of 720 aspects of the nityas in a year which is, of course the maximum sum of the longitude of the Sun and the Moon 720° (2 times 360°).

Following is the list of 27 yogas and certain characteristics associated with them:-

Table 9: Yogas and Longitudes

Number	Yoga	Longitude Sum of Sun and Moon
1	Vishkumbha Yoga*	0° to 13°20'
2	Priti Yoga	13°20' to 26°40'
3	Ayushman Yoga	26°40' to 40°00'
4	Saubhagya Yoga	40°00' to 53°20'
5	Shobhana Yoga	53°20' to 66°40'
6	Atiganda Yoga*	66°40' to 80°00'
7	Sukarma Yoga	80°00' to 93°20'
8	Dhriti Yoga	93°20' to 106°40'
9	Shoola / Sula Yoga*	106°40' to 120°00'
10	Ganda Yoga*	120°00' to 133°20'
11	Vriddhi Yoga	133°20' to 146°40'
12	Dhruva Yoga	146°40' to 160°00'
13	Vyaghata Yoga*	160°00' to 173°20'
14	Harshana Yoga	173°20' to 186°40'

Number	Yoga	Longitude Sum of Sun and Moon
15	Vajra Yoga*	186°40' to 200°00'
16	Siddhi Yoga	200°00' to 213°20'
17	Vyatipata Yoga*	213°20' to 226°40'
18	Variyan Yoga	226°40' to 240°00'
19	Parigha Yoga*	240°00' to 253°20'
20	Shiva Yoga	253°20' to 266°40'
21	Siddha Yoga	266°40' to 280°00'
22	Sadhya Yoga	280°00' to 293°20'
23	Subha Yoga	293°20' to 306°40'
24	Shukla Yoga	306°40' to 320°00'
25	Brahma Yoga	320°00' to 333°20'
26	Indra Yoga	333°20' to 346°40'
27	Vaidhriti Yoga*	346°40' to 360°00'

*Note: * -> Indicates Inauspicious Yoga.*

Vishkumbha Yoga : Natives born under this yoga are usually very beautiful and intelligent. They tend not to have any financial problems and are financially secure. Their birth yoga favours a happy family life. The natives of this yoga can easily influence people with their personality and have a big social circle. This yoga makes the natives very intelligent. Its ruling deity is said to be Yama.

Priti Yoga : Natives of this yoga as the name suggestswill be lively, inquisitive and work in a sporty spirit and are beauty worshipers. They are known to be popular with the opposite sex and they develop good relationship with them. They are clever and know how to achieve success in life. Its ruling deity is said to be Vishnu.

Ayushman Yoga : A native of this yoga will have a long life that means he/she will taste the happiness of life for a longer period in comparison to others. They are very fond of poetry and music, are born with wealth and do not face financial problems. They are physically strong and in a combat they have the capability to defeat enemies. Its ruling deity is said to be Soma or Moon.

Saubhagya Yoga : A native who is born with this yoga could end up with a great amount of fortune. People praise their qualities as they have various inborn talents in them. Its ruling deity is said to be Brahma.

Shobhana Yoga : A native born under this yoga is beautiful and attractive, and is known for his/her efficiency in executing any task assigned to him/her. His or her spouse will be very attractive and will possess good qualities, in addition to which the nativewill get a lot of satisfaction from progeny. Person born with this yoga may be slightly aggressive. Its ruling deity is said to be Brihaspati.

Atiganda Yoga : This yoga is counted amongst the inauspicious yogas. A native born with this yoga may cause difficulties and problems for his or her parents. The family could suffer on account of his/her temperament. Its ruling deity is said to be Chandra.

Sukarma Yoga : Natives born in this yoga are religious minded and involve themselves in such activities. They are excellent workers and have decent and simple nature. This yoga makes them compassionate and caring towards people. People usually love them for their behavioral qualities and kind-heartedness. Sukarma yoga gives the person a magnificent fortune. Its ruling deity is said to be Indra.

Dhriti Yoga : Natives of this yoga are very patient and don't get excited quickly and make their decisions only after giving things a long and hard thought. Normally, people of this yoga are talented and wise. They live a peaceful family life and achieve success in the society. Its ruling deity is said to be Apah or Jala.

Shoola / Sula Yoga : A person who is born in this yoga is known to have a religious nature. He may acquire great knowledge about religious things but he/she also has the material desire in him/her as this yoga makes him good in collecting wealth, too. However, it is also known to make the native lead an unhappy life, at times. Its ruling deity is said to be Sarpa or Naaga.

Ganda Yoga : People born in this yoga may lead a problematic life. They may have to face some real health problems in their life. Natives of Ganda yoga have a short stature with a big head. They are physically very strong and love to indulge in lavish activities. Its ruling deity is said to be Agni.

Vridhhi Yoga : Natives of this yoga have an attractive physique and a pleasing nature. This yoga gives prosperity and imparts some fine character traits in the native's nature. Additionally the character of the spouse and offsprings could also be outstanding. Its ruling deity is said to be Surya.

Dhruva Yoga : A person born in this yoga has a calm nature and a focused mind. This yoga gives physical strength along with an affluent life. The person gets love from almost every sphere of society for his/her composed nature and is blessed with a long life. Its ruling deity is said to be Bhumi.

Vyaghata Yoga : Persons born in this yoga are multi-talented and experts in doing various works. Their proficiency in multiple activities is appreciated in the society. They are very talented and skilled people and these characterstics aide them in achieving fame and success in their life. Its ruling deity is said to be Vayu.

Harshana Yoga : Natives of this yoga are considered to be fortunate. Their birth yoga makes them meritorious and scholarly in various subjects. They are grimly determined and have the fortitude to stand by their convictions and are well-respected in the socicty for these qualities. Its ruling deity is said to be Bhaga.

Vajra Yoga : The characteristic of this yoga is that it gives immense physical strength to its native. The physical power and the stamina which are obtained from this yoga make the native very skilled in physical endeavours. Vajra yoga makes its natives very courageous and strong. Its ruling deity is said to be Varuna.

Siddhi Yoga : If a person's yoga is Siddha yoga then he/she will be a multi-talented person. He/she has a dedicative and attentive nature and is normally capable of doing everything with equal skill. They have a charming and pleasing personality, are known to lead a happy life and also known to donate to the needy. This yoga can, however, cause health problems. Its ruling deity is said to be Ganesha.

Vyatipata Yoga : Slow and steady wins the race is the mantra for natives of this yoga. Natives born in this yoga experience a lot of difficulties in their formative years. Gradually, their experiences of life develop a unique quality of transforming sorrow into happiness. Slowly, but surely, they receive happiness and joyous moments and achieve success in life. Its ruling deity is said to be Rudra.

Variyan Yoga : Natives of this yoga are very artistic in nature and are good in music, dance and other art forms. They can achieve quick success if they try a career in these fields. The natives' interest in creative fields and the urge to perform in them is the specialty of this yoga. This yoga makes them strong and powerful individuals. Its ruling deity is said to be Kubera.

Parigha Yoga : The natives of this yoga are talented, wise, intelligent and possess knowledge of many subjects. With their varied knowledge they become famous and earn honour for themselves and their family. They are soft spoken and lead a happy life. Its ruling deity is said to be Vishwakarma.

Shiva Yoga : Native of this yoga are very intelligent and work for the welfare of the society. They seldom run after materialistic desires. They have a true heart and the inborn wisdom in their character gains respect from the society. Its ruling deity is said to be Mitra.

Siddha Yoga : People of this yoga have an attractive and an intelligent spouse and will also have enough wealth to live a comfortable life. Its ruling deity is said to be Karthikeya.

Sadhya Yoga : This yoga makes the character of the native determined and confident. Patience is a special characteristic trait in them and they wait for the fruits of their labour without much worry. Slow and steady wins the race is the name of the game for these people. Its ruling deity is said to be Savitri.

Subha Yoga : Natives who have this yoga are very beautiful, intelligent and talented. They have abundant wealth and never face any financial problem throughout the life. They are very generous donators and respect learned and religious people. Its ruling deity is said to be Lakshmi.

Shukla Yoga : Natives of Shukla yoga are expert in almost every art form. They are very fond of poetry and may become poets themselves in their own rights. They are very educated people and are endowed with great courage. Their birth yoga gives them financial security. Its ruling deity is said to be Parvati.

Brahma Yoga : People born in this yoga are known to be very proficient in multiple subjects. They have deep and abiding faith in God and possess a pious heart. Its ruling deity is said to be Ashwini Kumaras.

Indra Yoga : Natives born in this yoga are known to be very wealthy and carry some of the finest personality traits. They are known to lead a happy life. But this yoga has a malefic side as it may limit the longevity of the native. Its ruling deity is said to be Pitru Devas.

Vaidhriti Yoga : This yoga gives cheerfulness and positive energy to its native. Natives of this yoga perform the assigned task with a sporty spirit. This yoga will make the person very helpful and generous, but they may not get the credit they deserve for this. Its ruling deity is said to be Diti.

8

Karanas

A Karana is one-half of a tithi. We have already seen that one tithi ends at the moment of time when the angular distance between the Moon and the Sun becomes an integral multiple of 12°.

Given that a Karana is one-half of a tithi it is simply the time required for the angular distance between the Moon and the Sun to increase by 6°.

1 tithi = 2 karanas.

Given that there are 30 tithis constituting a Lunar month, there are sixty half-tithis or Karanas. The first Karana ends at the middle of the Tithi and the second Karana is extanded upto the end of that Tithi. The duration of each Karana under a tithi will be more or less equal.

1 Karana = Longitude difference of 6° between the Moon and the Sun.

A karana refers to a work or action that can be executed at a specified point in time. It refers to the day and night of a lunar day or tithi.

In terms of the above formula on tithis and karanas, there should be a total 60 karanas for the 30 tithis. In reality there are a total of 11 karanas out of which 4 are known to be fixed (sthira) in nature and occur only once in a lunar month while the remaining 7 are recurring or repeating (cara) in nature. Their occurrence has been provided in the table above. The 4 fixed karanas occur once in a lunar month while the 7 recurring karanas occur 8 times each in a lunar month.

Table 10: Karana and Tithi Mapping

Number	Shukla Paksha Tithi	1st Karana	2nd Karana	Number	Krishna Paksha Tithi	1st Karana	2nd Karana
1	Prathama	Kimstughna	Bava	16	Prathama	Balava	Kaulava
2	Dwitiya	Balava	Kaulava	17	Dwitiya	Taitula	Garija
3	Tritiya	Taitula	Garija	18	Tritiya	Vanija	Visti
4	Chaturthi	Vanija	Visti	19	Chaturthi	Bava	Balava
5	Panchami	Bava	Balava	20	Panchami	Kaulava	Taitula
6	Shashti	Kaulava	Taitula	21	Shashti	Garija	Vanija
7	Saptami	Garija	Vanija	22	Saptami	Visti	Bava
8	Ashtami	Visti	Bava	23	Ashtami	Balava	Kaulava
9	Navami	Balava	Kaulava	24	Navami	Taitula	Garija
10	Dasami	Taitula	Garija	25	Dasami	Vanija	Visti
11	Ekadasi	Vanija	Visti	26	Ekadasi	Bava	Balava
12	Dwadasi	Bava	Balava	27	Dwadasi	Kaulava	Taitula
13	Trayodasi	Kaulava	Taitula	28	Trayodasi	Garija	Vanija
14	Chaturdasi	Garija	Vanija	29	Chaturdasi	Visti	Sakuni
15	Poornima	Visti	Bava	30 (0)	Amavasya	Chatuspada	Naaga

Following is the list of 4 fixed and 7 recurring karanas and certain characteristics associated with them:-

4 Fixed Karanas

Sakuni Karana: A person born under this karana will be calm, composed, and intelligent, gifted with intuition and will be full of good deeds. This karana forms the 2nd half of the Krishna Paksha Chaturdasi tithi. Its ruling deity is Garuda. Another version states that its ruling deity is Kali.

Chatuspada Karana: A person born under this karana will do independent business, take great pains in work and will be truthful. This karana forms the 1st half of the Amavasya or New Moon Day. Its ruling deity is a bull (Vrishaba). Another version states that its ruling deity is Rudra or Shiva.

Naaga Karana: A person born under this karana will be of good moral character and will be an expert in multiple vocations. This karana forms the 2nd half of the Amavasya or New Moon Day. Its ruling deity is Naaga (serpent).

Kimstughna Karana: A person born under this karana is intelligent but may be bent on doing bad deeds. He could be unpopular and may suffer much in life. This karana forms the 1st half of the Shukla Paksha Prathama tithi. Its ruling deity is Kubera. Another version states that its ruling deity is Maruta.

7 Repeating Karanas:

Bava Karana: A person born under this karana might be poor but will be kind and content with whatever he gets. He might be successful in a career involving lots of physical work. Its ruling deity is Lord Vishnu. Another version states that its ruling deity is Indra.

Balava Karana: A person born under this karana will be handsome, courageous, sacrificing and will be interested in sporty activities. Its ruling deity is Brahma.

Kaulava Karana: A person born under this karana could be intent on doing bad deeds as his upbringing could have seen many hardships and an unhelpful ambience. Its ruling deity is Chandra. Another version states that its ruling deity is Mitra.

Taitula Karana: A person born under this karana will be soft hearted, even tempered and will possess strong convictions. Its ruling deity is Indra. Another version states that its ruling deity is Vishwakarma.

Garija Karana: A person born under this karana will be a good strategist, imaginative and talkative. Its ruling deity is Vasudeva. Another version states that its ruling deity is Bhumi.

Vanija Karana: A person born under this karana will have good business acumen and will be capable of succeeding in any type of business. Its ruling deity is Manibhadra. Another version states that its ruling deity is Lakshmi.

Visti Karana: A person born under this karana could be bent on doing bad deeds. Its ruling deity is Mrityu or death. It is also known as Bhadra.

9

Sun Signs

The sun sign as we have discussed is the position of the Sun in a particular zodiac at a particular date. The dates are assigned as per either the tropical or sidereal zodiac system given in table 1. A Sun Sign is the zodiac sign in your horoscope where Sun was in transit when you were born. We have already provided a brief description of the 12 zodiacs or rasis in the preceding chapters. Sun sign changes approximately once a month. Western astrology is based on sun signs. For example, if an individual were to be born on September 5, then irrespective of the time of the day per western astrology the individual would be a Virgo while he/she would be a Leo as per Vedic Astrology.

The Sun symbolizes your basic personality, the way life is approached and the factors contributing to your conscious day to day behavior. The Zodiac sign it occupies describes your character's essential qualities and your actions, and how you go about doing things. It exposes your personality to the outer world.

The Sun, by sign and house position, describes your ego's central traits and the sun sign, again, highlights your core personality. In conformity with western astrology, it is the most important sign of classification, but doesn't carry same importance in accordance with the principles enshrined in vedic astrology. The Moon and Ascendant signs are just as equally important and require an accurate birthday, place, and time. (The Sun changes signs approximately once a month. The Moon changes signs every 2.25 days. The Ascendant sign changes every 2 hours day after day after day.)

Sun sign forecasts can define what's happening for you on a conscious level and to your self-image.

10

Moon Signs

The moon sign is the position of Moon in a particular zodiac/rasi at a particular date and time. The Moon circles the Earth in approximately 27.32 days transiting 27 constellations or nakshatras which are mapped onto 12 rasis as we have discussed earlier. Each nakshatra lasts for approximately 24 hours with 2.25 nakshatras (or 2 nakshatras and 1 pada or quarter) mapping onto a single rasi (*See chapter on nakshatras).* Each rasi, therefore, lasts for approximately 54 hours or 2.25 days. Thus an individual's moon sign zodiac or rasi is simply based on the nakshatra and the corresponding rasi, the moon, is traversing at the time of his/her birth. As seen in our example from the chapter on sun signs, an individual born on September 5 would be sun sign Leo/Simha as per vedic astrology. If 2 individuals were born on this day their sun sign would be the same but if Individual 'A' was born at say 9 AM when the moon was transiting the nakshatras of Revati then his/her moon sign would be Meena (Pisces) whereas another individual 'B' was born at say 9 PM when the moon had moved across to the asterism or nakshatra of Ashwini then his/her moon sign or rasi would be Mesha (Aries). This example shows how moon transits across a single zodiac within 2.25 days as compared to the sun's transit once in 30 days. **Moon signs are critical in vedic astrology.**

In Astrology the Moon symbolizes your inner self, the part of you that responds from habit, feelings, and instinct. It is the way one's subconscious mind works. Moon thus is the planet or graha that rules over your mind. If you are a sensitive or emotional person, you may recognize your Moon sign qualities more readily than your Sun sign. These traits are who you are inside, or an intimate side of your character only of which you and those close to you really know. In fact, your moon sign may be very different from, or even in conflict with, your Sun sign traits. (Remember we have to judge an individual at the very least from both the moon and sun signs).

Forecasts based on your Moon sign reveal what's happening in your private life, your inner world, with your family situation and living conditions and how these things affect your mind and emotions. Because they target your experiences literally where you live you are apt to relate to readings that involve your Moon sign much more directly than those based on your Sun sign alone.

11

The 9 Planets (Navagrahas) of Vedic Astrology

Sun:

The Sun or Surya or Ravi or Aditya is foremost among the 9 celestial planets in vedic astrology. It is the king of all the 9 planets. Sun is the giver of life and soul of the universe, representing the life force which enlivens the solar system. It rules over our soul. The sun operates from the inner depth, illuminating the mind and soul, arousing spirituality and making the personality glow with radiance. Under the influence of sun, materialism, egotism and wrong-doing are eliminated. Outwardly determined and rigid, inwardly kind and royal, the sun operates majestically. Being such an overpowering planet, the effect of the sun is very significant. The sun gives us vitality and the power of resistance and immunity. It is responsible for our physical makeup. The sun gives life force, power of will, intellect, brilliance, prosperity, success in worldly affairs, wealth, personal conduct, activity, cheerfulness, good fortune, wisdom, ambition, fame and general understanding of the world.

Sun represents the male or father principle. He is considered the ruler of all 9 planets. He is a malefic planet given his hot and dry nature but also an auspicious planet. It owns the Leo / Simha zodiac / rasi which also happens to be its moolatrikona sign(0-20^0) and is exalted in Mesha or Aries (Exaltation @ 10^0 Aries). Its debilitation occurs at the polar opposite sign to Aries of Libra or Tula (10^0 Libra). It also owns 3 constellations or nakshatras Kritikka, Uttara Phalguni, Uttara Ashadha. The Sun's movement across the 12 zodiacs or rasis is always direct or clockwise.

As we have discussed in our chapter on Sun Signs, Earth takes 365.25

days or 12 months to make a complete revolution around the sun giving rise to the 12 zodiacs. As a result of this relative motion between the Earth and the Sun, the Sun stays in 1 zodiac for approximately 30 days (1 month). Sun is a star and the centre of our solar system. It is located at a distance of 1 astronomical unit or 150 million km from the Earth.

Given that the Sun is the centre of our solar system it signifies or is the significator of all the central themes of our life. Sun is the significator of our Father, Politics and Kingdom. It also signifies ability to go ahead, status of the native, religious inclination, courage, soul, forests and mountain peaks, energy, ambition, grace and personality.

Sun rules the Eastern direction and its ruling deity is Agni or Rudra. Its element is Fire and it governs greeshma ritu or summer. Sun is Saattwik in nature. Its colour is Gold.

Moon:

The Moon or Chandra is considered to be a planet of royalty in vedic astrology. Generally, the moon represents the mind and the emotions in a person, so has a very personal significance to each individual, whereas the sun represents the soul. The sun's light is reflected on the moon (as the moon has no light source of its own), so the moon is the bearer of the soul's energy. Therefore, the Moon indicates our emotional and psychological patterns and tendencies.The position and condition of the moon in the chart is crucial as it will show a lot about the character of the person and the tenor of their life. Given that the Moon is located closest to the Earth among all the 9 planets in vedic astrology it has the maximum amount of influence on an individual. Great value and importance are attached to an individual's moon sign or rasi in vedic astrology.

Moon represents the female or mother principle the energy that creates and preserves. The puranas however, state it to be a masculine planet given that it had 27 constellations as its wives. It is considered to be a royal planet. It is a natural benefic and an auspicious planet. It owns the Cancer / Kataka zodiac / rasi and is exalted in Vrishaba or Taurus (Exaltation @ 3^0 Taurus) which also happens to be its moolatrikona sign ($2\text{-}20^0$). Its debilitation occurs at Vrischika or Scorpio (3^0Scorpio). It also owns 3 constellations or nakshatras Rohini, Hasta and Shravana.

As we have discussed in our previous chapters, Moon takes ~27.3 days to make a complete revolution around the Earth. This gives rise to 27 nakshatras or constellations where the moon stays for about 24 hours each. Mapping these 27 nakshatras onto 12 rasis, the Moon stays in 1 zodiac or rasi for approximately 54 hours or 2.25 days. It is considered to be the fastest of all the 9 planets in vedic astrology.The Moon's movement across the 12 zodiacs or rasis is always direct or clockwise and it becomes combust when its longitude is less than or equal to 12^0 of that of the Sun. Moon is Earth's only natural satellite and is located at 384,400km away from Earth.

Given its feminine, royal, luminous and watery nature, moon signifies sense of purpose, illumination, intuitive nature, sensuality, liquids, sea travel, taste, youth, love of music and fine arts, jewelry, attractive appearance, wealth and good fortune.

Moon rules the North West direction and its ruling deity is Varuna or Gowri. It is a watery planet ruling over the tides of the sea and governs varsha ritu or the rainy season. Moon is Saattwik in nature. Its colour is Silver.

Mars:

The Mars or Mangal is said to be the commander-in-chief of the assembly of 9 planets in vedic astrology. It is the planet of war or the god of war. Being a warrior planet it is bile dominated by temperament. It rules over courage, bravery, patience, self-confidence and leadership abilities. Mars can make an individual short-tempered, argumentative, lover of weapons, commander, general, soldiers and policeman. It gives one technical and mechanical abilities.

Mars is a male planet and is the significator of siblings or co-borns. He is considered to be the commander of all the planets. He is a natural malefic but an auspicious planet. It owns the Aries / Mesha and Scorpio / Vrischika zodiac / rasi and is exalted in Capricorn or Makara (Exaltation @ 28^0 Capricorn). Its debilitation occurs at Kataka or Cancer (28^0 Cancer). Its moolatrikona sign is Aries or Mesha ($0\text{-}12^0$). It also owns 3 constellations or nakshatras Mrigashirsha, Chitra and Dhanishtha.

Mars takes ~687 days or approximately 2 years to make a complete revolution around the Sun. This means that it stays in 1 zodiac or rasi on an average for 45 days to 2 months. Mars' movement across the 12 zodiacs or rasis is generally direct or clockwise but once in about a couple of years it can also move in a retrograde or anticlockwise direction. During these periods Mars can stay in a house for a much longer period. Mars becomes combust when its longitude is less than or equal to 17^0 of that of the Sun. Mars is a planet of the solar system and is located at a distance of 54.6 million km from Earth.

Given Mars' nature of being a fiery planet with warrior like qualities, the planet is fond of law and order and arrangement. It gives energy, drive, determination, purpose, and great administrative ability and independent spirit. It signifies sportspersons, doctors and surgeons, politicians and administrative officers, military personnel.

Mars rules the South direction and its ruling deity is known as Subrahmanya, Murugan. It is a fiery planet and governs greeshma ritu or the summer season. Mars is Taamasik in nature. Its colour is Red.

Mercury:

Mercury or Budha is known to be the prince among the 9 planets in vedic astrology. Mercury is a moist planet which is gender neuter. As a result, it has a mercurial, quick changing and fickle nature. It is the smallest planet in our solar system. As a lord of Gemini it gives a double nature and makes one detached and independent as well as an extremist. Mercury causes youthfulness and immaturity. It is a good negotiator and stands for communication. It stands for thinking capacity and consequently, is known by the name of Budha. It enjoys the company of learned people.

Mercury is a convertible planet meaning it changes its gender based on the zodiac and the planet it co-habits with and is the significator of maternal uncle. He is considered to be the prince among all the planets. He is a natural benefic and an auspicious planet. It owns the Gemini / Mithuna and Virgo / Kanya zodiac / rasi and is exalted in Virgo or Kanya (Exaltation @ 15^0 Virgo). Its debilitation occurs at Pisces or Meena (15^0 Pisces). Its moolatrikona sign is Virgo or Kanya ($16\text{-}20^0$). It also owns 3 constellations or nakshatras Ashalesha, Jyestha and Revati.

Mercury is the fastest among all the tara grahas and takes 88 days to make a complete revolution around the Sun. It stays in 1 zodiac or rasi for approximately 1 month. Mercury's movement across the 12 zodiacs or rasis is generally direct or clockwise but it can also move in a retrograde or anticlockwise direction more often than other planets excepting rahu and ketu. Longitude of Mercury is always less than or equal to $27^0$of that of the Sun. This means it can at the most be positioned 1 zodiac or rasi away from the Sun in a rasi chart. It is the planet closest to the Sun in a rasi chart. Mercury becomes combust when its longitude is less than or equal to 14^0 of that of the Sun when direct, and $12^0$when retrograde anticlockwise. Mercury is a planet of the solar system and is located at a distance of 77 million km from Earth. It is the planet closest to the Sun in the Solar System.

Being an effective communicator Mercury stands for education, writers, lecturers, artists, teachers, traders, businessmen, and rules intelligence, speech, self-confidence, humour, wit, astrology, mathematics and short journeys, engineering, computers and technology, accountancy.

Mercury rules the North direction and its ruling deity is Lord Vishnu. It is an earthy planet and governs hemanta ritu or the season of dew. Mercury is Raajasik in nature. Its colour is Green.

Jupiter:

Jupiter or Guru or Brihaspati is known to be the teacher of the gods in vedic astrology. It is the largest planet in our solar system. He is the advisor or teacher of demi-gods. Given its weight Jupiter tends to expand things (e.g. Body weight, Speech, Financial worth, Family, Progeny). It is the best benefic. It bestows upon the affected individuals knowledge, good fortune, wisdom, good growth in all walks of life. It is the best adviser.

Jupiter is a male planet and is the significator of children. He is considered to be the greatest benefic among all the 9 planets. He is a natural benefic and an auspicious planet. It owns the Sagittarius/ Dhanus and Pisces / Meena zodiac / rasi and is exalted in Cancer or Kataka (Exaltation @ 5^0 Cancer). Its debilitation occurs at Capricorn or Makara (5^0 Capricorn). Its moolatrikona sign is Sagittarius or Dhanus ($0\text{-}10^0$). It also owns 3 constellations or nakshatras Punarvasu, Vishaka and Purva Bhadrapada.

Jupiter is the largest planet in the solar system and takes 12 years to make a complete revolution around the Sun. As a result, it stays in 1 zodiac or rasi for approximately 1 year. Jupiter's movement across the 12 zodiacs or rasis is generally direct or clockwise but it can also move in a retrograde or anticlockwise direction. Jupiter becomes combust when its longitude is less than or equal to 11^0 of that of the Sun. Jupiter is a planet of the solar system and is located at a distance of 588 million km from Earth.

Jupiter signifies higher education, knowledge, priest, spiritual teacher, minister, adviser, legal system and law, banking and financial services, religion, philosophy, faith, excess, guide, luck and fortune and long distance travel.

Jupiter rules the North-East direction and its ruling deity is Indra or Brahma. It is an ether (space) planet and governs seeta ritu or the winter season. Jupiter is Saattwik in nature. Its colour is Yellow.

Venus:

Venus or Shukra is the planet of beauty, grace and refined things that are desirable. It is also the planet of materialistic desires. Shukra is the son of Bhrigu Maharishi but also the teacher of anti-gods or asuras. It is an embodiment of love, refined attributes, romance, sensuality, passion, comforts, luxuries, jewellery and wealth, decoration, art, music, dance, rains.

Venus is a female planet and is the significator of spouse. She is a natural benefic and an auspicious planet. It owns the Taurus / Vrishaba and Libra / Tulazodiac / rasi and is exalted in Pisces or Meena (Exaltation @ 27^0 Pisces). Its debilitation occurs at Virgo or Kanya (27^0 Virgo). Its moolatrikona sign is Libra or Tula(0-15^0). It also owns 3 constellations or nakshatras— Bharani, Purva Phalguni and Purva Ashadha.

Venus takes approximately 225 days on average to make a complete revolution around the Sun. It stays in 1 zodiac or rasi for about a month on average. Venus' movement across the 12 zodiacs or rasis is generally direct or clockwise but it can also move in a retrograde or anticlockwise direction. Longitude of Venus is always less than or equal to $48^0$of that of the Sun. This means it can at the most be positioned 2 zodiacs or rasis away from the Sun in a rasi chart. Venus becomes combust when its longitude is less than or equal to 10^0 of that of the Sun when direct and 8^0 when retrograde. At its furthest, Venus often is called Earth's twin planet in the solar system, and is situated at a distance of 261 million km from Earth.

Venus signifies feminine spirit, beauty, grace, enjoyment, taste, love, sexuality, charm, refinement, vanity, charisma, glamour, media and entertainment, cinema, drama, poetry, music, dance, and theatre.

Venus rules the South-East direction and its ruling deity is Sachi Devi or Indrani. It is a watery planet and governs vasanta ritu or the spring season. Venus is Raajasik in nature. Its colour is White/Yellow.

Saturn:

Saturn or Shani or Shanaishchara the 'slow mover' is a cold, dry, elderly and lethargic planet. It is known as the planet of the masses or the common man. It is the planet that is the farthest away from the Sun among the navagrahas. It is the son of the Sun god. It is said to be the most malefic among malefics. Saturn is also known to be the greatest bestower of boons as it signifies practicality and realism. Despite being feared, Saturn is known to provide wisdom, integrity, spirituality, fame, patience, ability to lead, authority, long life, organizational abilities and development, keen awareness of right and wrong, sincerity, honesty, and love of justice. As it is a slow moving planet, it is also known to occasion delays, sorrows, dejection, obstruction, defensiveness, secretive behaviour, and nervousness.

Saturn is a female planet and is the significator of longevity. She is a natural malefic and an inauspicious planet. It owns the Capricorn / Makara and Aquarius / Kumbha zodiac / rasi and is exalted in Libra or Tula (Exaltation @ 20^0 Libra). Its debilitation occurs at Aries or Mesha (20^0 Aries). Its moolatrikona sign is Aquarius or Kumbha ($0\text{-}20^0$). It also owns 3 constellations or nakshatras Pushya, Anuradha and Uttara Bhadrapada.

Saturn is the second largest planet and the most distant planet from the Sun in the solar system, and takes 30 years to make a complete revolution around the Sun. Consequently, it stays in 1 zodiac or rasi for approximately 2.5 years. Saturn's movement across the 12 zodiacs or rasis is generally direct or clockwise but it can also move in a retrograde or anticlockwise direction. Saturn becomes combust when its longitude is less than or equal to 15^0 of that of the Sun. Saturn is located at a distance of 1.2 billion km from Earth.

Saturn signifies participation in mass production involving large work force, low technology industry, leadership of labour/industrial workers, service, discipline, structure, order, concentration, the masses.

Saturn rules the West direction and its ruling deity is Brahma or Yama. It is an airy planet and governs sisira ritu or the autumn season. Saturn is Taamasik in nature. Its colour is Blue/Black.

Rahu + Ketu:

Rahu and Ketu are shadow planets or chaaya grahas of vedic astrology. Rahu and Ketu were both known to have been born to Demon Viprasitthi and his wife Simmikai. The story goes that long ago there was a great war between the Asuras (demons) and Devas (gods). The Devas were routed in the war and they went to Lord Brahma to seek his help. Brahma told them to churn the ocean. As a result, they would be able to obtain Amrit (nectar), which would make them immortal and all powerful, and after consuming it they would be able to defeat the Asuras. Churning the ocean was a great task and so the Devas sought the help of the Asuras. The king of the serpents Vasuki was to become the rope, while a hill named Mandrachal offered to become the pivot. Lord Vishnu, in the form of a tortoise (Kurma) which is also the second avatar of Vishnu became the base and the churning process began.

The Devas held the tail of Vasuki and the Asuras held the head. Various things came out, during this churning of the ocean. There was a pot of Vish (poison) which created havoc in all the three worlds. Lord Shiva drank the poison to save the world, but he did not let the poison go beyond his neck which became blue in colour. That is why Lord Shiva is also called 'NeelKant' (*"one with a blue neck"*).

At last Dhanvantari came out with a pot of Amrit and immediately there was a mad scramble for it among the Devas and Asuras. Seeing this, Lord Vishnu took the form of Mohini (a beautiful dancer) and offered her services in distributing the Amrit equally to both the Asuras and Devas. She made both of them sit in two different rows but she gave the Amrit to the Devas only. Towards the end, one of the Asuras saw through her trick. He went and sat among the Devas and drank the Amrit. The moment Chandra (Moon) and Surya (Sun), who were sitting beside him, saw that he was an Asura, they informed Mohini. Lord Vishnu came in his real form and let out the Sudarshan Chakra (wheel) at the Asura. The Asura's neck was separated from the body, but he did not die as he had drunk the Amrit. His head was called 'Rahu' and his torso 'Ketu'. Thus were born the 2 grahas or planets of Rahu and Ketu. Rahu is the planet of materialistic desires and speculation and gambling tendencies. Its nature is that of anger, anxiety, and suddenness. It signifies fame, extremes, foreigners and foreign lands, fulfilment of worldly desires, status, prestige, power, success, obsessions, addictions, psychics, poisons that destroy and heal, drug dealer, alcohol, magicians. Ketu, despite being a malefic, is the planet of spirituality and salvation. It is also known as moksha-karaka. It can bestow wisdom, powers of discrimination and spiritual knowledge. It gives one psychic ability. For a materialistically minded person it can turn out to be a very damaging planet much more so than Saturn and Rahu. It signifies loss, liberation, perception, wisdom, lack of confidence, negation, self doubt, fantasies, drug addiction, alcoholism, injury, spiritual insight.

Rahu owns 3 constellations or nakshatras Ardra, Swati and Satabishak while Ketu owns Ashwini, Magha and Moola. In a rasi chart Rahu and Ketu are always 180^0apart. For e.g. if Rahu's ecliptic longitude is 100°, then Ketu' ecliptic longitude would be 100+ 180 or 280^0. Simply put, if Rahu is in Mesha then Ketu would be in the 7th sign from Rahu which is Tula. Although there are multiple versions of Rahu and Ketu's exaltation, own and moolatrikona signs/zodiacs we will not discuss these as it is still a subject matter for protracted debate and acceptable conclusion. Rahu and Ketu are the Northern and Southern or Ascending and Descending Nodes of the Moon which also go by the names of dragon's head and dragon's tail. Their movement across the 12 zodiacs or rasis is always in retrograde or anticlockwise direction. Given that they are mathematical points they are never combust.These two nodes of the Moon's orbit move in sync with each other, in a retrograde motion, due to the action of the Sun's gravity on the Moon's motion, and they make a complete circuit or revolution in ~18 years. As a result, they stay in 1 zodiac or rasi for approximately 1.5 years.

Rahu rules the South West direction. Rahu's ruling deity is Durga/Nirrti while Ketu's is Ganapati/Chitragupta. Rahu and Ketu are said to be Taamasik in nature. Rahu's colour is Dark Blue, while Ketu's is Smoky Grey.

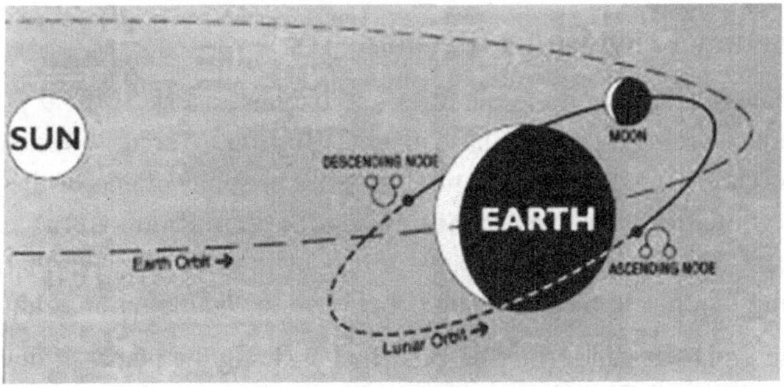

Figure 4: The nodes of the Moon (Rahu and Ketu)

12

Planetary Terminologies

Planetary Friendships (Permanent):

We have already seen the qualities and characteristics of the 9 planets in vedic astrology. Four of these planets **(Jupiter, Mercury, Venus and Moon)** are termed as being natural benefics or subha grahas or the good guys while the other five are **(Sun, Mars, Saturn, Rahu, Ketu)** termed as being natural malefics or papa grahas or the bad ones. Furthermore waxing moon is termed as being benefic while waning moon is not.

These 9 planets can further be classified as being the planet of devas or daitya (asuras). The planets of **Sun, Moon, Mars and Jupiter** are the planet of the **devas** while **Saturn, Venus, Rahu and Ketu** are the planet of the asuras. **Mercury** is **neutral**.

Among these planets exists friendship, enmity and neutrality. These relationships are permanent or natural in nature and can affect the functioning of planets in a native's rasi chart. Deva planets are generally friendly with one another while asura planets maintain healthy relationship amongst one another. Mercury is generally friendly with all.

Table 11: Planetary Friendships (Permanent)

Planet	Friends	Neutrals	Enemies
Sun	Moon, Mars, Jupiter	Mercury	Saturn, Venus
Moon	Sun, Mercury	Mars, Jupiter, Venus, Saturn	None
Mars	Sun, Moon, Jupiter	Venus, Saturn	Mercury
Mercury	Sun, Venus	Mars, Jupiter, Saturn	Moon
Jupiter	Sun, Moon, Mars	Saturn	Mercury, Venus
Venus	Mercury, Saturn	Mars, Jupiter	Sun, Moon
Saturn	Mercury, Venus	Jupiter	Sun, Moon, Mars

It can be seen from the above table that friendships among individual planets is not 2-way in nature. For example, Moon is friendly to Mercury whereas Mercury hates the Moon.

Retrograde:

Retrograde planets or vakri grahas as they are termed in vedic astrology are those planets of the Solar System other than the Sun, and the Moon that appear to move backwards. We all know that different planets in the solar system have different orbital periods around the Sun. The 3 outer planets of Mars, Jupiter and Saturn have a longer orbital period when compared to Earth. As a result, the Earth passes by or overtakes the outer planets periodically which cause the outer planets to appear to move backwards. This phenomenon is called retrograde motion, which invariably occurs at a time when that planet is visible for a relatively longer period and the earth is between the sun and that outer planet. In reality the planet is not moving backward but there is a difference in relative motion of the planet w.r.t Earth which causes it to appear as being in retrograde motion. Think about 2 cars "A" and "B" traveling at 60 KMPH on a highway and suddenly "A" accelerates and starts traveling at 90 KMPH. It will appear to "A" that "B" is moving backwards although in reality "B" is moving forward albeit at a speed slower than that of "A". The two inner planets of Mercury and Venus which are closer to the Sun when compared to Earth also retrograde due to their conjunctions with the Sun. A planet in retrograde motion is closer to the Earth than is normal.

Astronomically speaking, when a planet goes from perihelion (the part of a planet's orbit nearest to the Sun) to aphelion (the part of a planet's orbit most distant from the Sun) as it recedes from the Sun, it gradually loses the power of the Sun's gravitation and, consequently, to gain it, it retrogrades. When the planet comes from aphelion to perihelion the gravitational pull of the Sun is powerful and the planet starts to accelerate and appears to move in a direct or clockwise manner for an observer on earth.

Out of the 9 planets in vedic astrology the Sun and the Moon are always direct in motion and are never be retrograde. Think about the fact that June always comes after May and not the other way around. In a similar manner Purva Phalguni always precedes Uttara Phaguni and not the other way around. Kanya rasi always follows Simha Rasi and Tula Rasi always follows Kanya Rasi. The 2 mathematical nodes or illusionary planets Rahu and Ketu always move in a retrograde or anticlockwise manner. The remaining 5 planets which we term as tara grahas are generally direct but will periodically turn retrograde like rahu and ketu.

Table 12: Retrograde Motion of Planets

Planet	Retrograde Frequency	No. of Days of Retrograde	Longitudinal Difference from Sun
Jupiter	Once a Year (Every 399 days)	~120 days	~115° (245°)
Saturn	Once a Year (Every 378 days)	~140 days	~108° (252°)
Mars	Once every 2 years (Every 780 days)	~60-80 days	~130-140°
Mercury	3 Times a Year (Every 116 days)	~21-25 days	Variable
Venus	2 Times in 3 Years (Every 584 days)	~42 days	Variable

Note: Slight variation in numbers on days and longitude can be expected based on the almanac used.

Planets in retrograde motion (especially the tara grahas) are given much importance due to their ability to alter astrological observations and predictions. It is said that retrograde planets become very powerful and their ability to do good or bad can be enhanced. A planet in exaltation but in retrograde is as good as a debilitated planet while a planet in debilitation but retrograde is as good as being exalted. Vakri grahas can give very unexpected results. One can also say that a planet in retrograde motion is akin to it being on a vacation which can postpone the occurrence of a positive or negative event.

Combust:

Combust planets and asta graha is a term used to signify planets in vedic astrology losing their radiation or light emitting capabilities or getting burnt when they go very close to the Sun. The Sun is known to be the giver of life and is considered pure in nature but is not a natural benefic because life cannot be sustained on the Sun as it burns or combusts any entity including planets when it goes near the Sun. Given that the concept of combustion is derived from the Sun, the Sun itself can never become combust. The shadow planets of Rahu and Ketu which are, physically speaking, mathematical points can also never be combust. The remaining 6 planets become combust as described in the table below.

Table 13: Planetary Combustion

Planet	Combustion Frequency	No. of Days of Combustion	Longitudinal Difference from Sun
Moon	Once a Month	1-2 days	12°
Jupiter	Once a Year	~30 days	11°
Saturn	Once a Year	36 days	15°
Mars	Once every 2 years	100-120 days	17°
Mercury	7 Times a Year (Combust 50% of the Year)	12-15/25-30/45-50 days (Direct), 12-18 days (Retrograde)	14° (Direct), 12° (Retrograde)
Venus	Once or Twice a Year	~80 days (Direct), 5 - 10 days (Retrograde)	10° (Direct), 8° (Retrograde)

On account of their close proximity to the Sun these planets are not visible at night, after sunset or before sunrise. A classic example of this is the New Moon or Amavasya day when the Moon is not visible.

In a combustion state a benefic loses part of its power to do good, while a malefic becomes even more malignant. At the end of the combustion period the planet or graha resumes its light emitting capabilities or is uday.

When a planet becomes combust, it becomes weak by combustion and thus it becomes unable to protect its significances fully and produce proper results unlike a planet which is not combust and is capable of producing proper results.

Moolatrikona / Exaltation / Debilitation / Own Sign:

We have briefly touched upon the concepts of exaltation, debilitation, and moolatrikona of the planets. What do these positions of the planets signify? Basically, these positions provide us with a view on relative strengths of a planet when posited in the 12 zodiac signs or rasis. Planets, like human beings, also possess a comfort zone whilst traversing across the 12 zodiacs. One school of thought defines these terminologies as given below.

A planet when placed in its own house (not the Moolatrikona) is akin to being at its own home, comfortable, relaxed and peaceful.

A planet when placed in its Moolatrikona spot is akin to being at its workplace being fully sincere and committed to the function it is to perform. This is the zodiac where a planet feels itself to be very responsible.

A planet when placed in exaltation sign is akin to being at its favourite party or a place doing their most favourite thing and enjoying thoroughly.

A planet when placed in debilitation is the exact opposite. It hates this place, feels uncomfortable wants to get away but is stuck.

A planet placed in its friend's or enemy's house will accordingly feel more or less comfortable on a moderate level when compared to it being in a sign of exaltation or debilitation.

According to the Kalidasa authored Uttara Kalamrita which is considered to be an important landmark in the history of vedic astrology, the relative strength of a planet in various signs is:-

Exaltation Sign = 1 Rupa

Moolatrikona Sign = 0.75 Rupas

Own Sign = 0.5 Rupas

Adhi Mitra Sign = 0.375 Rupas (Natural friend + Temporary friend)

Friend Sign = 0.25 Rupas(Temporary friend + Natural neutral) Neutral Sign = 0.125 Rupas (Temporary friend + Natural enemy) (Temporary enemy + Natural friend)

Enemy Sign = 0.0625 Rupas (Temporary enemy + Natural neutral)

Adhi Shatru Sign = 0.03125 Rupas (Temporary enemy + Natural enemy)

Rupa here is defined as a unit of measurement to calculate the relative strength of a planet. It is the numeral one.

Planetary Conjunctions And Aspects:

Two planets placed in the same zodiac sign or rasi are said to be in conjunction. For example, if Jupiter and Venus are placed in Tula they are said to be conjunct. Conjunct planets in a horoscope can alter the outcome of potential results(positive or negative) as one planet which is more powerful, could influence the behavior of the other. In reality, a conjunction is more powerful and pronounced when the longitudinal difference between the planets in conjunction is negligible or very less. A conjunction of Mercury and Saturn in 29^0Scorpio and 2^0Sagittarius is more powerful when compared to a conjunction of the same 2 planets in 3^0Leo and 27^0Leo as the longitudinal difference in the former would be 3^0whilst in the latter it would be 24^0.

A planet "A" is known to fully aspect or look at another planet "B" when the 2 planets are exactly opposite to each other (they are in the 7th house from each other) in a birth chart. The 7th house aspect is a 2-way relationship as "B" will also aspect "A". An aspect of one planet on another can once again alter the results that the second planet is likely to confer on an individual.

According to the Bhrigu Samhita:-

Six planets Sun, Moon, Mercury, Venus, Rahu and Ketu fully aspect the 7th sign from where they are placed in a horoscope.

Mars, in addition to fully aspecting the 7th sign, also aspects the 4th and 8th signs clockwise from where it is placed in the horoscope.

Jupiter in addition to fully aspecting the 7th sign also aspects the 5th and 9th signs clockwise from where it is placed in the horoscope.

Saturn, in addition to fully aspecting the 7th sign, also aspects the 3rd and 10th signs clockwise where from it is placed in the horoscope.

Given their longer orbital periods and large size the aspects of Jupiter, Saturn and Mars are considered to be more significant. The aspect of Jupiter in general is considered very auspicious while that of Mars and Saturn is considered to be negative. Of course one must examine the relative position of these planets in the rasi chart as well as their position in a particular rasi and house before arriving at any conclusion.

Significator and Dispositor Planets:

A **Significator** planet (also known as karaka) is a planet that signifies indicates or rules over a specific thing or issue. For example, if an individual is born in Tula (Libra) Lagna then owner of that native's 1st house is Venus. The 1st house indicates oneself or how the native perceives the world to be. A Tula Lagna individual would have Venusian like qualities (e.g. Artistic in appearance and outlook).

If the native's Lagna is Kumbha or Aquarius then the 2nd house would be Meena or Pisces and its ruler Jupiter. Second house is the indicator for wealth and Jupiter here would be the primary determinant for how such an individual accumulates wealth or otherwise in life.

A **Dispositor** planet is a planet in whose sign another planet is located in the rasi chart. For example, If Venus is located in Kataka or Cancer, then Moon who is the owner of this zodiac is termed as the Dispositor planet for Venus. It is said that a strong and favourably placed dispositor will enhance the strength of the planet(s) occupying its sign. This is especially true in case of Rahu and Ketu which, according to certain astrological texts do not own any sign. If Rahu is, say placed in Gemini or Mithuna, and Mithuna Lord Mercury is exalted in Kanya (Virgo), then Rahu could give spectacular results to the individual for whom Rahu is placed in Mithuna in his Rasi Chart. If, on the other hand, Mercury is debilitated in Meena (Pisces), then Rahu could yield very unfavorable results.

Planetary Gunas:

Many of us would know that guna signifies a quality in any being. According to one school of Hindu philosophy there are 3 primary gunas Saattwik, Raajasik andTaamasik. Saattwik guna is known to maintain purity, balance, and order. This is when the mind is steady, calm and peaceful and free from any attachment to the result. Ancient and modern rishis are known to be saattwik. Raajasik which could be connected to the word raja is a quality of dynamism, enthusiasm, being actionable or excitable and initiating change. It is considered to be less positive than saatwik. Taamasik indicates inertia or being too lethargic, dull or slow and indifferent and resisting action. It is considered to be less positive than raajasik.

Hora:

The **Hora** as we have already stated literally means the quality of time. The Hora is a one hour duration in a day, ruled by a particular planet. On each day of the week starting from Sunday each of the 7 classical planets rules a one hour period from sunrise to sunset and again from sunset to sunrise. Given that there are 12 zodiacs, and day and night there are a total of 24 horas and 24 hours in a day. Depending on the ruling planet the horas are either suitable or unsuitable for various undertakings. For example, the Hora of Venus is used for selecting the muhurtha for marriage.

We have already seen the time taken by each of the planets to make 1 revolution around their respective orbits. In descending order of orbital periods this would be:-

Saturn -> Jupiter -> Mars-> Earth -> Venus -> Mercury -> Moon

Moon which is considered as a planet in Vedic astrology has the fastest orbital period.

Replacing Earth with Sun we get:-

Saturn -> Jupiter -> Mars-> Sun -> Venus -> Mercury -> Moon

Rearranging the above order of planets starting with Sun we get:-

Sun -> Venus -> Mercury -> Moon -> Saturn -> Jupiter -> Mars

Given that the Sun is the king of all planets and the day starts after sunrise, as per the Hindu almanac the first day of the week Sunday is named after the Sun.

If we follow the above order each of the above planets will rule for an hour. So the Sun rules the 1st Hora on Sunday, Venus the 2nd, Mercury the 3rd and so on. The 21st Hora is ruled by Mars, 22nd by Sun, 23rd by Venus and 24th by Mercury. Twenty four horas complete a day and the 25th Hora - which marks the sunrise of the following day - is ruled by Moon or Monday. In a similar manner, we can see that Mars rules

Tuesday, Mercury Wednesday, Jupiter Thursday, Venus Friday and Saturn Saturday.

Hindu Calendar:

The Hindu calendar is a luni-sidereal calendar that has been used extensively in India since ancient times. There are some variations in this calendar, given the number of languages present in the country, but I will share the most common version that is used by panchangams and astrologers.

The list of 12 months as per the Hindu calendar is as follows:-

1. Chaitra (Chitra) (Mar-Apr)
2. Vaisakha (Vishaka) (Apr-May)
3. Jyestha (Jyeshtha) (May-Jun)
4. Asadha (Purva Ashadha) (Jun-Jul)
5. Sravana (Shravana) (Jul-Aug)
6. Bhadrapada (Purva Bhadrapada) (Aug-Sep)
7. Ashvina (Ashwini) (Sep-Oct)
8. Kartika (Krittika) (Oct-Nov)
9. Margasirsa (Mrigashirsha) (Nov-Dec)
10. Pausha (Pushya) (Dec-Jan)
11. Magha (Magha) (Jan-Feb)
12. Phalguna (Uttara Phalguni) (Feb-Mar)

The naming convention for these months is based on the nakshatra (in brackets) that falls on the full moon or Poornima day of that month. For example, during the month of Chaitra the full moon day will occur on the day when Moon is traversing the Chitra constellation. Given that this is a lunar calendar there will be variation in the dates used by the Gregorian calendar (months given in brackets). There are 2 popular versions of this calendar. One is the Amanta Calendar where the first day of each month is the first day after the new moon (Amavasya) day. The other is the Purnimanta Calendar which starts with the first day following the full moon (Poornima) day. Each month consists of 29 or 30 lunar days (Tithis) comprising of Shukla Paksha and Krishna Paksha.

The Hindu calendar consists of 60 Samvatsaras (Sanskrit term for 'year'). Once the 60 samvatsaras are over, the cycle repeats itself.

13

Ascendant / Lagna

We often hear the term Ascendant or Lagna or Rising Sign and the significance that it carries when casting a horoscope of an individual. What exactly is a lagna? Quite simply the Lagna is the zodiac or rasi that is rising in the eastern horizon of the sky when an individual takes birth. When casting a horoscope, an individual's birth chart consists of 12 houses. The 1st house of the rasi chart is the Lagna and from it follows the remaining 11 houses (2nd through 12th) in clockwise direction. The Lagna is the single most important facet in judging the relative strength of a horoscope. It determines the placement of planets in the 12 houses and their lordships (more on this in the next chapter) which, ultimately, aides in predicting future outcomes. This lagna is also referred to as the Udaya Lagna.

How do we go about obtaining the Lagna of an individual? As we mentioned earlier the lagna is the zodiac rising in the eastern horizon of the sky at the time of the birth. It is, therefore, connected to the position of the Sun (The planet that rules the eastern direction) in the sky at the time of the birth. The Sun as we know stays approximately for 30 days or a month in 1 zodiac. If we assume a sunrise time of 6 AM and if the Sun is posited in the zodiac of Leo or Simha (Sidereal Zodiac Please!!!) then the rising sign or lagna is also Leo / Simha. Given that there are 24 hours in a day and 12 zodiac signs or rasis, the lagna changes approximately every 24/12 or 2 hours on an average. As a result birth at 6AM could mean the lagna is Simha while birth at 8AM could mean Lagna is Kanya and birth at 10AM could mean Lagna is Tula.

Table 14: Sample Lagna Chart for an individual born during the sidereal zodiac of Leo (Aug-Sep) with sunrise at 6AM:

Time of Birth	Lagna
6AM	Simha
8AM	Kanya
10AM	Tula
12PM	Vrischika
2PM	Dhanus
4PM	Makara
6PM	Kumbha
8PM	Meena
10PM	Mesha
12AM	Vrishaba
2AM	Mithuna
4AM	Kataka

We have already seen that the rising periods for the 12 rasis vary even at the equator and difference only increases as we move away from the equator. As a result, the lagna rarely changes exactly once in 2 hours or 120 minutes. It could change once in 90 minutes or once in 150 minutes but the average time spent across each of the 12 zodiacs over a single day is 2 hours. For an accurate calculation of the Lagna, one would require the latitude and longitude of the location, date and the time of birth.

Now that we know that the lagna is calculated based on position of Sun in a specific zodiac and the time of birth, we can also figure out the placement of Sun in a particular house. Given that the Sun moves slowly across a single zodiac, relative to the rising sign during any particular day, while the lagna keeps moving in a clockwise manner roughly every 2 hours, a day birth (post sunrise) would indicate that the Sun is placed in houses 7 through 12 in an individual's birth chart, while a night birth (post sunset) would indicate that the Sun is placed in houses 1 through 6. A sunrise birth indicates Sun being invariably placed in the 1st house while a sunset birth would indicate Sun being placed in the 7th house.

As the 1st house is known as the ascendant house the 7th house is termed as the descendant house. Birth at local noon or mid-day when the Sun is at its highest point indicates the Sun being placed in the 10th house. Similarly, birth at midnight indicates the Sun being placed in the 4th house.

Let us now examine a couple of methods for calculating the lagna.

Vedic Method of Calculating Lagna

The following steps are used in obtaining the lagna:-

1. Obtain the Nirayana Longitude of Sun at sunrise for the specified location on the specified date (This information will be available in any Hindu almanac or panchang).
2. Add the Ayanamsa value to obtain the Sayana Longitude of sunrise.
3. Find out the difference in time between the time of birth and time of sunrise on the given day in ghatis and vighatis. It is advisable to use the Local Mean Time(LMT) for both the times. Birth-Sunrise Time Difference = ((LMT(Time of Birth) – LMT (Sunrise)) *2.5) (In Ghatis)
4. Find out the rising sign at sunrise from step 2 (eg: If Sayana Longitude = 250° then rising sign at sunrise is Sagittarius).
5. Subtract the nearest previous multiple of 30° from this Sayana Longitude to obtain remainder degrees to be traversed in the current sign (eg: 280°-250°= 30°). Remainder Degrees = Nearest next multiple of 30° - Sayana Longitude.
6. Identify the hemisphere and latitude of the location. For Northern Hemisphere the signs Cancer through Sagittarius are signs of Long Ascension while the signs Capricorn through Gemini are Short Ascension signs. Obtain the charkhanda values from table 1 in appendix for the latitude of the location.
7. Calculate adjusted rasimana for the 3 groups of signs listed in table 4. Convert this number into Ghatis and Vighatis. Adjusted Rasimana = Rasimana +- Charakhanda in Asus (+ for Long Ascension, - for Short Ascension)
8. Calculate the Remainder Time in Rising Sign. Remainder Time in Rising Sign = (Remainder Degrees / 30°) * Adjusted Rasimana for Rising Sign at Sunrise (In Ghatis)

9. Add the adjusted rasimana for the following sign.

10. Repeat step 9 till the sum of adjusted rasimanas exceeds time difference obtained in step 3 (e.g.: If time difference is 25 ghatis then the adjusted rasimana sums must not exceed 25 ghatis). The sign where the sum exceeds the time difference is the Tropical Ascendant or Lagna.

11. Sayana Longitude of Lagna = (30° / Adjusted Rasimana for Tropical Lagna Sign) * (Time Difference –Sum of Adjusted Rasimanas prior to Tropical Lagna Sign).

12. Nirayana Longitude of Lagna = Sayana Longitude of Lagna - Ayanamsa

Trigonometric Method of Calculating Lagna

The following trigonometric formulae can also be applied in calculating the Lagna. Please note that the following method is used in obtaining the sayana longitude which then must be reduced to its nirayana equivalent by deducting the ayanamsa.

1. R = arctan ((sin (H) * tan (L)) / (cos ((sidereal time*15°) + H)))

2. Sayana Longitude of Cusp = arctan ((cos (R) * tan ((sidereal time*15°) + H))/ (cos (R + E)))

3. Nirayana Longitude of Cusp (Including Lagna) = Sayana Longitude of Bhava Madhya - Ayanamsa

In the above formulae:-

H:This is the degree in multiples of 30 starting from the 10th house (H=0 for 10th house, H=30° for 11th house etc.). For the calculation of Lagna H=90°.

L: Latitude of the location

E: Obliquity of the ecliptic for the given year

Arctan is inverse tan function.

Please refer to Appendix III for further information on sidereal time.

Example 5:

Calculate the ascendant or lagna for an individual born on **Friday, August 15, 2014 @ 2:30PM (14:30), New Delhi, India.**

Let us use the vedic method for calculating the lagna. As per western or tropical astrology, Sun is in Leo on August 15th.

Note from table 15 that a birth at 2:30 PM some 8-9 hours after sunrise means that 4 or 5 signs (average of 2 hours per sign) would have been traversed since sunrise meaning that the lagna is likely to be Scorpio or Sagittarius.

Nirayana Longitude at Sunrise = 118°04'(See Chapter on Panchangam and Timekeeping).

Sayana Longitude at Sunrise = Nirayana Longitude + Ayanamsa = 118°4' + 24°3' = 142°7'.

Local Mean Time at Sunrise = 5h33m (See Panchangam and Timekeeping).

Local Mean Time at Birth = 14h30m – 21m = 14h9m.

Birth-Sunrise Time Difference = 14h9m - 5h33m = 8h36m or 8.6 hours = 8.6 * 2.5 = 21.5 ghatis.

Sayana Longitude of 142°7' means rising sign is Leo (120-150 degrees).

Remainder Degrees = Nearest next multiple of 30° - Sayana Longitude = 150° - 142°7' = 7°53'

New Delhi's latitude is 28°36'north. Let us take the charakhanda values provided in table 1 of Appendix 1 for 28° in Asus.

Charakhanda 1 = 382.8, Charakhanda 2 = 306.24, Charakhanda 3 = 127.6.

We already know the rasimana values at equator for the 3 groups of signs:-

I	Aries	Virgo	Libra	Pisces	1674
II	Taurus	Leo	Scorpio	Aquarius	1795
III	Gemini	Cancer	Sagittarius	Capricorn	1931

Given that Delhi is in the northern hemisphere the signs of long ascension will be Cancer through Sagittarius while the signs of short ascension will be Capricorn through Gemini. We accordingly calculate the adjusted rasimanas by applying the above charakhandas. Adjusted Rasimanas:

Aries, Pisces = 1674-382.8 = 1291.2 Asus = 3.587 Ghatis

Taurus, Aquarius = 1795-306.24 = 1488.76 Asus = 4.135 Ghatis

Gemini, Capricorn = 1931 – 127.6 = 1803.4 Asus = 5.0 Ghatis

Cancer, Sagittarius = 1931 + 127.6 = 2058.6 Asus = 5.718 Ghatis

Leo, Scorpio = 1795 + 306.24 = 2101.24 Asus = 5.837 Ghatis

Virgo, Libra = 1674 + 382.8 = 2056.8 Asus = 5.713 Ghatis

Remainder Time in Rising Sign = (7°53' / 30°) * 5.837 = 1.534 Ghatis

Adjusted Rasimana for Virgo = 5.713 Ghatis

Adjusted Rasimana for Libra = 5.713 Ghatis

Adjusted Rasimana for Scorpio = 5.837 Ghatis

Adjusted Rasimana for Sagittarius = 5.718 Ghatis

Sum of adjusted rasimanas for Leo, Virgo, Libra and Scorpio = 18.797 (< 21.5)

Sum of adjusted rasimanas for Leo, Virgo, Libra, Scorpio and Sagittarius = 22.982 (> 21.5)

Thus, the tropical ascendant is Sagittarius

Sayana Longitude of Lagna = (30° / 5.718) * (21.5-18.797) = 14.18° Sagittarius or 254.18°

Nirayana Longitude of Lagna = 254.18° - 24.06° = 230.12° or 230°7' or 20°7' Scorpio or Vrischika

Thus, the Lagna at birth is Vrischika or Scorpio and its longitude is 230°7'.

We have already discussed the difference between the sun and moon signs in our previous chapters. Where does the Lagna fit into the scheme to things in judging the characteristics of an individual? The key difference here lies in the fact that since Lagna is based on the time of birth it indicates how an individual would see and approach the world through the lens of his eyes.Your Ascendant describes your temperament, the lens through with you view the world, the personality you put on public display. It's the side of your character you willingly show the outside world. It is how the world views you and your mental and physical characteristics. While the sun sign changes once a month and moon sign changes once in 2.25 days, ascendant changes once in 2 hours. This explains the fact why even people born on the same day can have very different personalities, different strengths and interests, and different life experiences.The Lagna quite simply indicates an individual's physical appearance and complexion, mental characteristics, nature of birth, fame and defame and success. It is an indicator of an individual's body, mind and soul.

As the ascendant changes more frequently when compared to moon and sun signs forecasts based on the ascendant will be the most descriptive and accurate regarding life circumstances and immediate future. One can relate to such information very readily which makes the Ascendant sign information even more crucial than that based on Sun or Moon sign.

The characteristics or qualities of individuals born under the 12 zodiacs would resemble that of the 12 moon sign rasis. Specific characteristics of the 12 rising signs are described belows.

Mesha (Aries) Lagna:

Individuals born in mesha lagna are lovers of scientific thought. They are enterprising and ambitious. They have the ability to plan. They dislike being guided by others; are intense when interested, vehement when excited. They are rather stubborn, but often frank. Quick tempered, they resent imposition and are liable to go to extremes. Their constitution will be hot. They love beauty, art and elegance. They are liable to suffer from diseases of the head depending on the birth chart.They are independent thinkers, courageous and sensitive, middle stature, ruddy complexion, sharp sight, long face and neck, head broad at temples and narrow at chin, brown or light and curly, mark or scar on the head or temples, teeth well-set and round eyes.

Vrishaba (Taurus) Lagna:

If they are not listened to attentively, people born in this sign will act like a bull. They are self-reliant. They have their own principles and ways, and a piercing intellect. They have a great deal of endurance, power and latent energy. They always put their ideas into practice. Their physical prowess and mental endurance are indeed noteworthy.

They are fond of pleasure. They love beauty and music. They possess a magnetic personality. They think they are born for exercising authority. They generally suffer from nervous complaints after the 50th year. With regard to children much happiness is not indicated. They are obstinate, proud and ambitious, easily accessible to adulation but affectionate and loving, sometimes unreasonable, prejudiced and stubborn. The stature of the person born in this sign will be short and often tending towards corpulence, lips thick and complexion swarthy, square build of the body, face beautiful, eyes and ears large, full forehead, hands plump and broad.

Mithuna (Gemini) Lagna:

They are very active and tend to become experts in mechanical sciences. They may suffer sudden nervous breakdowns. They must be cautious in moving with opposite sex. Their mind will often be conscious of their own depravity. They are very clever and possess inherent conversational and literary ability. They are liable to fraud and deception and can have deceitful and tricky nature if evil planets are present in Gemini. They are the best in occupations where there is much activity.They will have a wavering mind and are fond of writing and reading, ingenious and quick witted, vivacious and inconsistent, nervous and restless. They are tall and straight in stature and active in motion with face well developed, there is a depression near the chin, a thin face, sanguine complexion, unusual height if malefics are there, eyes are clear and the nose snub. They are weak but active.

Kataka (Cancer) Lagna:

They are very intelligent, bright and extremely frugal and equally industrious. Their frugality often takes the form of miserliness. The mind is intuitional, perceptive. They like pleasure. They are deeply attached to their family and children. They often meet with disappointment in love affairs. They are very talkative, self-reliant, honest and unbending. They will have a reputation for love of justice and fair play. Their emotions are strong. They have psychic tendencies, are receptive to new ideas and adapt themselves to environment. They are desirous of possessions and cautious. They can best take up occupations of a fluctuating nature. People born in this sign will be extremely sensitive, inquisitive, nervous and restless, interested in music and dexterous. They have a middle sized body, face full, slightly snub nose, fair complexion, long arms, long face and wide chest.

Simha (Leo) Lagna:

They can adapt themselves to any condition in life. They have faith. In affection they are sincere. They stick to orthodox principles in religion but are perfectly tolerant. Generally good tempered they are sensitive. They are lovers of music, literature and possess a certain amount of philosophical knowledge. They are voracious readers. In life they often do not succeed as much as they would like to and often struggle very much. Their ambitions remain unfulfilled to a great extent. They lack natural policy and hence, get into many difficulties. They are forgiving and do not hold a grudge for long. They are likely to suffer from nervous troubles and are generally misunderstood by their superiors. People born in Leo are ambitious as well as avaricious, warm-hearted, and have a liking for art, literature and music. They are cheerful and unimpulsive. Persons born in this sign will be magnetic in appearance with broad shoulders, bilious constitution with average height, oval faced, thoughtful countenance and the upper part of the body is generally well formed.

Kanya (Virgo) Lagna:

They exhibit their intelligence when quite young. They are discriminating and emotional and get carried away by impulse. They are cautious regarding their own interests, prudent, economical, diplomatic and shrewd. As authors they make progress in physical and chemical sciences. They acquire much power and influence over others. They are of speculative nature and, at times, are prone to suffer from nervous breakdowns. Those born in Virgo are impulsive, emotional and fond of learning. They love music and fine arts. They lack self-confidence. Methodical and active, they have active minds. Persons born in this sign will be middle-sized. Their chest will be prominent and could, at times, be weak also. They have a straight nose, cheeks massive and the forehead, good.

Tula (Libra) Lagna:

People born in this sign are generally of a sensual disposition. They are keen observers of human nature. They have keen foresight and reason out things from the standpoint of their own views. They love justice, peace, order and are agreeable persons. They are ambitious. They are more idealists than realists or practical men and often contemplate on schemes that are like castles building in the air. They are not sensitive to what others say of them. As political leaders and religious reformers they exert tremendous influence over the masses and sometimes their zeal and enthusiasm can go to such a pitch that they can force their views upon unwilling minds. They are not easily amenable to reason. They are great lovers of music. Truth and honesty have a special appeal for them. Persons born in libra are idealistic, quick-witted, vindictive, forceful and positive. They generally possess fair complexion, a middle-sized stature, phlegmatic constitution, handsome appearance, broad face, fine eyes, broad chest and regular features. Their appearance will generally be youthful.

Vrischika (Scorpio) Lagna:

They will have a generous disposition. They are exceedingly fickle-minded and love much excitement. Though inclined to sensual things in reality, they will not hesitate to philosophize upon the virtues of controlling sensual pleasures. They are good correspondents. They are often brutal, brusque and keenly fond of contest. They possess enterprise. They appreciate luxury but are frugal. They may become expert musicians if they learn the art. They can become proficient in fine arts, dancing and the like. They uphold their own views. Their constitution will be hot and they are likely to suffer from piles. They are good conversationalists as well as writers and rely on their intelligence. Sarcastic and impulsive, a female born in this sign will be masculine in nature. Interested in occult forms of study they possess a subtle mind and are hard to influence. Persons born in this sign are handsome in appearance. The bones are well developed. They have broad eyes, tall figure and curly hair and broad forehead. The personality is forceful with prominent brows and perceptive faculties.

Dhanus (Sagittarius) Lagna:

They are of a phlegmatic temperament. They are too conventional and also business-like. They are prompt and uphold conservative views. They are sympathetic and loving and possess good foresight. At times, they are restless and over-anxious. They are too callous and enthusiastic. They hate all external show. They are god-fearing, honest, humble and free from hypocrisy. They exercise strict control over their food and drinks and in regard to their relations with the opposite sex. They are prone to being misunderstood unintentionally by others. They must be careful about their lungs. Those born in Sagittarius have an inclination to philosophy and occult studies. They can acquire great mastery in these subjects. Humane and impulsive, they are generally active and enterprising. Persons born in this rising sign are generally inclined towards corpulence. They possess almond eyes and there is brown. They are usually good looking. They have an evenly set teeth and a happy smile.

Makara (Capricorn) Lagna:

They have a knack to adapt themselves to circumstances. They have great aspirations in life and cannot economize funds. They like a lot of show, are noted for their perseverance. They can become vindictive and could become bigoted. They are capable of much endeavor. On the domestic front they are perfectionists and often cannot get along well with husbands or wives. They should check this harmful tendency on their part. They are industrious. They can be described as chatter-boxes and have little control over their tongues. Occasionally, they could be funky, nervous and weak-minded. They are stoical to the miseries of life. Possessed of sympathy, generosity and philanthropy, self-willed, strong in purpose, secretive and vindictive they are cunning and determined. Persons born in this sign are tall, lean, reddish-brown in colour with prominent stiff hair on the eyebrows and the chest. The head is big and the face fairly broad. They have a large teeth, a big mouth, prominent nose, and are inclined to stoop. The body is thin and fleshy.

Kumbha (Aquarius) Lagna:

They make friends of others very soon. They can rise like a bulldog but their anger can also easily subside. They shine very well as authors and writers and their conversation is always interesting. They are sometimes timid and funky. They feel shy to exhibit their talents in front of a new audience. They could specialize in subjects such as astrology. Their literary greatness comes before the world at a young age. They could suffer from critical setbacks which can affect their reputation. They are prone to be misunderstood. In family life they will not have sufficient happiness. They might not have sufficient happiness in family life and are liable to suffer from colic troubles and chest pain. People born in this sign become great teachers, lecturers and writers. They are philosophical in nature. They are reserved, peevish when provoked, generous hearted, highly sympathetic and bent on helping others. They are intelligent and have good memory. They are generally tall and lean with countenance, handsome, appearance attractive and disposition elegant. Their lips are flushy, cheeks are broad and they have prominent buttocks and temples. The chest could be weak.

Meena (Pisces) Lagna:

They respect orthodoxical principles and can forgo anything but orthodoxy.They are extremely superstitious. They are very reserved and are liable to draw premature conclusions on any matter. They are god-fearing and very rigid in observance of religious customs and practices. They are stubborn, rather timid and ambitious to exercise their authority over others. They rarely realize their ambitions. They are restless and fond of history, antiquarian talks and mythological masterpieces. They are frugal in spending money and though generally dependent upon others throughout their life, still bear a mark of independence. They are just in their dealings and fear to transgress the laws of truth.Persons born under this sign are stubborn, psychically receptive, highly religious, stoical, bigoted and god-fearing. They are fair, stout of middle-sized height, swarthy in complexion, eyes 'piscean' and inclined towards corpulence.

FUNCTIONAL BENEFICS + MALEFICS

In the previous chapter we touched upon the concept of natural benefics and malefics among the 9 planets. We also touched upon friendships that exist among these planets and their power to do good or bad based on the zodiac that they sit in a rasi chart. While the concepts associated with these benefics and malefics hold good for one and all there also exist functional benefics and malefics for a rasi chart based on the lagna. Each lagna has planets disposed towards it favourably, unfavourably or neutrally based on its planetary ruler or lord, natural friendships among the planets and the 12 houses of a rasi chart.These planets are the functional benefics and malefics of the lagnas. We will elaborate on the significance of the 12 houses in the following chapter but a brief overview on their nomenclature below.

The 1st(house of lagna), 5th and 9th houses are known as trikona or trines. They are also termed as Lakshmi Sthanas and thus are considered auspicious/fortune granting houses.

The 1st, 4th, 7th and 10th houses are known as kendras or quadrants or the angular houses. They also go by the term Vishnu Sthanas given their ability to confer status and position in society.

The 2nd, 5th, 8th and 11th houses are known as the succedent houses meaning following.

The 3rd, 6th, 9th, 12th houses are known as apoklimas or cadent houses meaning falling or decline.

The 3rd, 6th, 10th and 11th houses go by the term upachayas meaning increase.

When judging the functional benefic or malefic nature of the planets, the following rules hold good:-

1. Lords of the 1st, 5th and 9th houses are functional benefics for any lagna with the 9th being the best benefic followed by 5th.
2. Lords of the 3rd, 6th and 11th houses are functional malefics for any lagna with the 11th being the worst malefic followed by the 6th.
3. Lords of the 4th, 7th and 10th if they happen to be natural benefics become functional malefics. It should also be stated that a natural benefic owning a quadrant and sitting in the same quadrant ceases to be a malefic. For e.g.: If the lagna happens to be kanya, then Jupiter owning the 4th and 7th houses will turn a functional malefic. It will, however, cease to be a functional malefic if it occupies the 4th or 7th house in the birth chart.
4. Lords of the 4th, 7th and 10th if they happen to be natural malefics become functional benefics. It should also be stated that a natural malefic owning a quadrant and sitting in the same quadrant ceases to be a benefic.

5. Neutrals in a horoscope include: Moon when he is the lord of the lagna; the Sun or the Moon as the 8th lord; the Sun or the Moon as the lords of the 2nd and 12th.
6. Rahu and Ketu are not included in the list of functional benefics and malefics given the argument that exists on their ownership over any zodiac.

Table 15: Lagnas + Functional Benefics and Malefics

Lagna (Ascendant)	Functional Benefics	Functional Malefics	Neutrals
Aries (Mesha)	Jupiter, Mars, Sun	Mercury, Saturn, Venus	Moon
Taurus (Vrishaba)	Saturn, Mercury, Mars, Sun	Jupiter, Moon	Venus
Gemini (Mithuna)	Venus	Mars, Jupiter, Sun	Moon, Mercury, Saturn
Cancer (Kataka)	Mars, Jupiter	Venus, Mercury	Saturn, Moon, Sun
Leo (Simha)	Mars, Sun	Mercury, Venus	Jupiter, Moon, Saturn
Virgo (Kanya)	Venus	Moon, Mars, Jupiter	Saturn, Sun, Mercury
Libra (Tula)	Saturn, Venus, Mercury	Sun, Moon, Jupiter	Mars
Scorpio (Vrischika)	Moon, Jupiter, Sun	Mercury, Venus	Mars, Saturn
Sagittarius (Dhanus)	Mars, Sun	Venus, Saturn, Mercury	Jupiter, Moon
Capricorn (Makara)	Venus, Mercury, Saturn	Mars, Jupiter, Moon	Sun
Aquarius (Kumbha)	Venus, Sun, Mars	Jupiter, Moon	Mercury, Saturn
Pisces (Meena)	Mars, Moon	Saturn, Sun, Venus, Mercury	Jupiter

Given that 5 tara grahas own 2 rasis or zodiac they will lord over 2 houses. When a planet lords over a Kendra (Vishnu sthana) and a trikona (Lakshmi sthana) it is said to be the yogakaraka planet for that lagna. A yogakaraka planet confers fame, honour, dignity, financial prosperity, political success and reputation. This is possible only in case of the following 6 lagna's:

Vrishaba Lagna ->Yogakaraka: Saturn -> Lords over 9th and 10th house

Kataka Lagna ->Yogakaraka: Mars -> Lord over 5th and 10th house

Simha Lagna ->Yogakaraka: Mars -> Lords over 4th and 9th house

Tula Lagna ->Yogakaraka: Saturn -> Lords over 4th and 5th house

Makara Lagna ->Yogakaraka: Venus -> Lords over 5th and 10th house

Kumbha Lagna ->Yogakaraka: Venus -> Lords over 4th and 9th house

One can observe that the yogakaraka planet for the 6 lagnas is a great friend of the lord of that lagna.

14

12 Houses of A Rasi/Birth Chart

(How to Construct Your Birth Chart / Horoscope)

We have briefly touched upon the 12 houses ('Bhava' in Sanskrit) of a birth/rasi/natal chart in the previous chapters. The first house of a birth chart is the lagna and in clockwise fashion follow the remaining 11 houses. For instance, If the lagna is Simha, then the 2nd house is Kanya, 3rd Tula and so on up until 12th house which is Kataka.

These 12 houses signify the different aspects of an individual including but not limited to Birth, Education, Profession, Marriage, Death, Significant Relationships, Residence, Travel & Journeys etc.

Let us examine each of these 12 houses.

1st House / Thanubhava / House of Self:

The 1st house is the house of oneself. It is the lagna or nature of our birth. It is how we perceive the world or what the world thinks of us. It signifies physique, will-power, fame, figure and physical complexion/ appearance/colour/constitution/beauty/stature, success. The significator planet of this house is the Sun. Its direction is east which follows from the fact the lagna is the zodiac rising from the eastern horizon of the sky at the time of birth.

2nd House / Dhanabhava / House of Wealth:

The 2nd house signifies the constitution of the face and vision, vocal ability, finance, family life, wealth, speech, treasure and bondage. It is one of maraka or death inflicting houses. The significator of this house is Jupiter.

3rd House / Bhratrubhava / House of Siblings, Courage and Communication:

This is the house of our siblings, energy, ability to undertake physical and mental workload, warriorship, courage and risk taking ability, leadership ability, communication skills, ears and throat. The significator is Mars.

4th House / Sukhabhava / House of Home and Family:

This is the house of the mother, motherly relations, elementary education, comforts, land and buildings, real estate and conveyances, mental strength, peace and happiness, places of rest, heart. The significators are Moon and Mercury. Its direction is north.

5th House / Putrabhava / House of Children, Creativity and Entertainment:

This is the house of children, knowledge, wisdom, faith in god, creativity and entertainment, speculation, advisory. It is also known as the poorvapunya sthana or house of past karma.The significator is Jupiter.

6th House / Satrubhava / House of Health, Debt and Enemies:

This is the house of enemies, diseases, debt, accidents, regression, diligence, occultism, maternal grandfather, defeats and victories, stomach. The significators are Mars and Saturn.

7th House / Kalatrabhava / House of Marriage and Partnerships:

This is the house of the spouse, marriage, business partnerships and co-operation. As this house is the polar opposite or 180^0away from the ascendant, it also goes by the term the descendant. It is one of maraka or death inflicting houses. It also signifies anything non-habitual or foreign to an individual. The significator is Venus. Its direction is west.

8th House / Ayurbhava / House of Longevity:

This is the house of age and longevity, occult and dark sciences, inheritance, legacies and gifts, daily routine, career and troubles, degradation, private parts of the body. The significator is Saturn.

9th House / Dharmabhava / House of Dharma:

This is the house of righteousness, destiny, dharma, philosophy, religion, higher education, fortune, father figure, teacher or guru or preceptor, intuition, divine power and fame, fame, charities, leadership, long distance journeys or foreign travel. This is the house of Dharma (Some include the 1st and 5th house in this list). The significators are Jupiter and Sun.

10th House / Karmabhava / House of Profession:

This is the house of ability, occupation, splendor, sovereignty, government, social status, prestige and honour, dignity. This is the house of Karma or Artha (Some include the 2nd and 6th house in this list). It also goes by the name of the midheaven house. Many consider this to be the most important house in a birth chart. An individual born at local noon or mid-day will have the planet of Sun placed in the 10th house of his/her birth chart. The significators are Jupiter, Sun, Saturn, Mercury. Its direction is south.

11th House / Labhabhava / House of Gains:

This is the house of friendships, wealth, income and gains, acquisition, realization of wishes, prosperity, and fulfilment of necessities.This is the house of Kama (Some include the 3rd and 7th house in this list). The significator is Jupiter.

12th House / Vyayabhava / House of Losses:

This is the house of expenditure, losses, sorrows, poverty, contact of foreign places, pleasures of the bed, emancipation or salvation. This is the house of Moksha (Some include the 4th and 8th house in this list). The significator is Saturn.

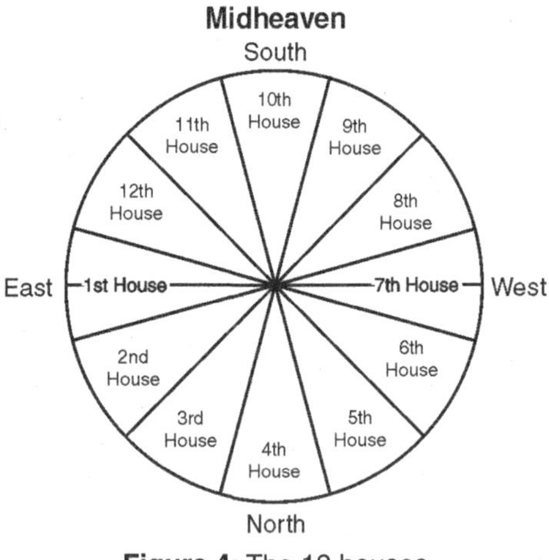

Figure 4: The 12 houses

The placement of planets in a rasi chart in a particular rasi and house determine its individual strength and its relative equation with the other 8 planets. We have already seen that the 1st, 5th and 9thhouses are termed as the lakshmi sthanas or fortune giving houses. The natural benefics of Jupiter, Mercury, Venus and Moon work well and attain sthana balam in these houses while the natural malefics of Sun, Mars, Saturn, Rahu and Ketu feel uncomfortable here. Likewise the lords of the 3rd, 6th and 11th houses are termed as malefics as a result of which the natural malefics perform well in these positions while natural benefics feel challenged. Of course the fact that the 11th house indicates gains and 3rd house indicates courage means even natural benefics would carry some positives when posited in these houses. The 4 kendra sthanas or seat of powers i.e. houses 1,4,7 and 10 need to be analyzed carefully before arriving at any conclusion. We have already discussed their house ownership by natural benefics and malefics.

The planets of Sun and Mars attain digbali or directional strength when facing south or the 10th house.Intuitively, Sun is present in the 10th house at mean noon or mid-day when it is directly over the head and is at its most potent self. Mars is the planet of war and action and the 10th house rules over our vocation and profession as a result of which Mars becomes powerful here.

The planets of Moon and Venus attain digbali when facing north or the 4th house. The 4th house represents our home, comfort zone and peace which is where the Moon is at its best given its royal nature. Additionally the Moon is powerful at night much like how the Sun is powerful during the day. Venus also feels powerful in this house of happiness, peace, heart and comfort as it represents luxury, comforts and merry.

The planets of Jupiter and Mercury attain digbali when facing east or the 1st house. Jupiter represents Knowledge and Wisdom while Mercury represents Communication, Skill and Intellect both of which are critical to an individual's personal growth. It is the 1st house or Lagna that best represents how we perceive the world and how the world perceives us which explains the digbali for these two planets.

The planet of Saturn attains digbali when facing west or the 7th house. This is quite straightforward given that Saturn represents the masses or the common man and 7th house being the opposite of the 1st house signifies co-operation, partnerships, collaboration all of which are foreign to an individual in any undertaking.

Planets in digbali give good wealth, prosperity, happiness and fame to the native during its periods or sub-periods.

Moon, Mars and Saturn are strong in the night time. Sun, Jupiter and Venus are strong in the daytime. Mercury is neutral but strong during sunrise or sunset.

Natural malefics are strong in Krishna paksha. Natural benefics are strong in Shukla paksha.

Natural malefics are strong in Dakshinayana. Natural benefics are strong in Uttarayana.

In judging the strength of a rasi chart the following 8-point theorem is to be applied with great care:-

1. Lagna and the Lord of the Lagna
2. Placement of the 9 planets in various rasis (Exaltation Sign, Debilitation Sign, Own Sign, Friend's Sign, Enemy's Sign, Neutral Sign)
3. Placement of planets in various houses from the Lagna
4. Position of the Moon and its strength as well as the position of the planets relative to the Moon.
5. Conjunction of various planets in a sign
6. Aspects of planets on various signs/houses and other planets
7. Position of all planets relative to each other in the birth chart as well as their natural and temporal friendship/enmity/neutrality.
8. Relative strength of the divisional charts (eg: Navamsa chart)

Planetary Friendships (Temporal):

In the previous chapter we discussed the natural friendships among the non-illusionary planets. The 9 planets also have **temporal friendships** and enmity amongst themselves based on their relative position in an individual's birth chart based on the following criteria:-

1. Two planets 'A' and 'B' are temporal friends if both the planets are placed in the same sign or in the second and twelfth, or third and eleventh, or fourth and tenth from each other.Some people consider two planets in the same sign to be temporal enemies.

2. Two planets 'A' and 'B' are temporal enemies if both the planets are placed in the opposite signs (180^0 apart), or in the sixth and eighth, or fifth and ninth from each other.

3. The relationship is mutual (2-way) unlike in the case of natural friendships.

4. There is only friendship and enmity in temporal relationships and no neutrality.

Friendship between 2 planets must be judged using both natural and temporal relationship. Natural relationship is obviously given more weightage.

Rasi /Birth/Natal Chart Pictorial Representation:

The following is a pictorial representation of a rasi chart in both the North as well as the South Indian system (Planets in bracket are the sign rulers).

South Indian Chart:

12 Meena (Jupiter)	1 Mesha (Mars)	2 Vrishaba (Venus)	3 Mithuna (Mercury)
11 Kumbha (Saturn)			4 Kataka (Moon)
10 Makara (Saturn)			5 Simha (Sun)
9 Dhanus (Jupiter)	8 Vrischika (Mars)	7 Tula (Venus)	6 Kanya (Mercury)

North Indian Chart:

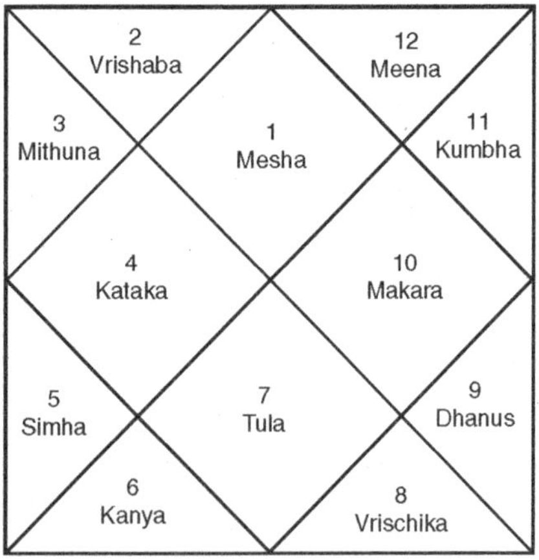

Example 6:

Pictorial representation of a lagna chart for a native born under **Simha Lagna**

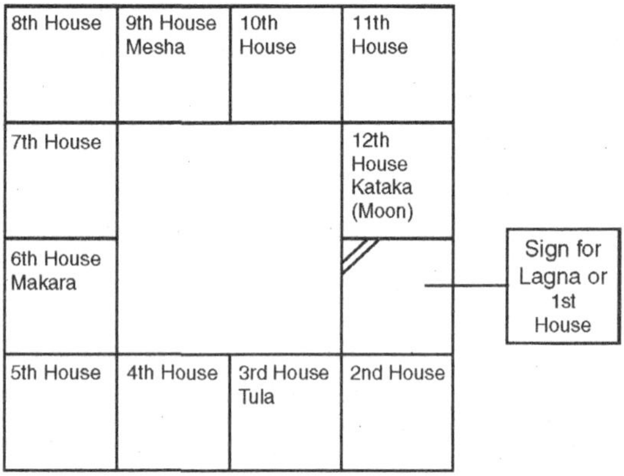

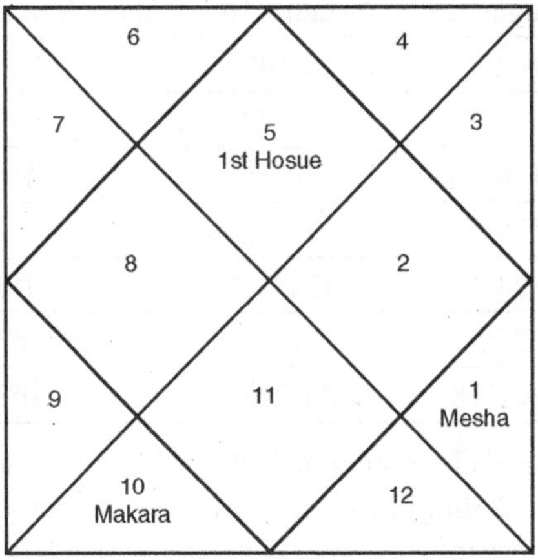

Example 7:

Compute the rasi chart of a native born on **Friday, August 15, 2014 @ 2:30PM (14:30), New Delhi, India**.

We have already computed the lagna for a native born at the above time in the previous chapter.

Lagna = 230°7' (Vrischika or Scorpio)

From table 1 we can figure out that Sun is placed in Kataka or Cancer sidereal zodiac.

There are multiple methods of computing the planetary longitudes with very high levels of accuracy. We will apply a relatively simplistic yet highly accurate approach which takes into account the daily motions of the planets. Most Hindu almanacs (panchangs) and ephemerides give the position of all the 9 planets at a specified time of the day for all days of the year. One such panchang has been used to obtain the information below.

Sayana Longitudes of the Planets at 5:30AM IST on August 15th, 2014 and 16th August 2014 respectively:-

	August 15	August 16	Daily Motion of the Planet
Sun	142°7'	143°4'	0°57'
Mars	221°7'	221°42'	0°35'
Mercury	148°40'	150°35'	1°55'
Jupiter	126°32'	126°45'	0°13'
Venus	123°17'	124°31'	1°14'
Saturn	227°9'	227°12'	0°3'
Rahu	202°18'	202°15'	0°3'

We now have the daily motion of 7 planets over a 24-hour period. The time of birth of 2:30PM IST means that 9 hours have elapsed since 5:30AM on August 15th.

Daily Motion of a Planet = Sayana Longitude (Day 2) – Sayana Longitude (Day 1) (At the same time)

Longitude of a planet at the time of birth = Sayana Longitude of the planet on the first day + ((Daily Motion of the Planet / 24) * (Time interval between birth time and the time at which the longitude of the planet is listed in the ephemeris on the first day)) (We subtract in case the planet moves in a retrograde manner as is always the case with Rahu and Ketu)

Applying the above formula we obtain the following sayana longitudes:-

Sun = ((0°57'/24)*9) + 142°7' = 142.47°

Mars = ((0°35'/24)*9) + 221°7'= 221.33°

Mercury = ((1°55'/24)*9) + 148°40'= 149.38°

Jupiter = ((0°13'/24)*9) + 126°32'= 126.61°

Venus = ((1°14'/24)*9) + 123°17' = 123.74°

Saturn = ((0°3'/24)*9) + 227°9' = 227.16°

Rahu = 202°18'((0°3'/24)*9) = 202.28°

The above are sayana longitudes. We will, of course, need the nirayana longitudes which can be arrived at by subtracting the ayanamsa value (24.06 on August 15th2014 as seen in chapter 2)

The Nirayana Longitudes of the planets are:-

Sun = 118°24' (Kataka)

Mars = 197°16' (Tula)

Mercury = 125°19' (Simha)

Jupiter = 102°33' (Kataka)

Venus = 99°41' (Kataka)

Saturn =203°6' (Tula)

Rahu = 178°13' (Kanya)

Ketu = 178°13' + 180° = 358°13' (Meena)

The above formula for calculating the nirayana longitude works well for Moon also but given the gravitational force that exists between Earth and Moon the daily arc traversed by Moon might be subject to minor fluctuations, as a result of which the above formula might be subject to an error of a minute or two. Consequently, for calculating the position of the Moon, we use the formula from appendix IV.

Moon = 1°57' (Mesha)

The daily motion of Sun over the 24 hour period between August 15th and 16th is 0°57'. Additionally, we know that the Sayana Longitude of Sun at 5:30AM IST on August 15th is 142°7'. These two data points will help us in calculating the position of Sun at any point of time on August 15th.

Sayana Longitude of Sun at 6AM on August 15th = 142°7' + ((0°57'/24)*0.5)

Nirayana Longitude of Sun at 6AM on August 15th = 142°7' + ((0°57'/24)*0.5) – 24.06 = 118°04'

This is, of course, the number that we used in calculating the sunrise time using the Hindu method in the chapter on panchangam and timekeeping.

The rasi chart of such a native using the aforementioned longitudes would look like this.

Rasi Chart

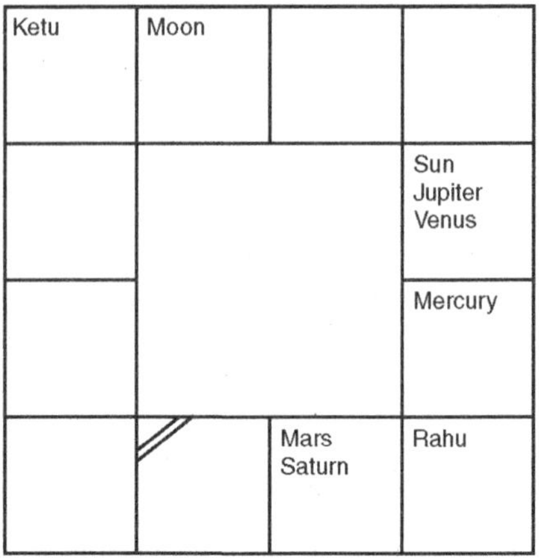

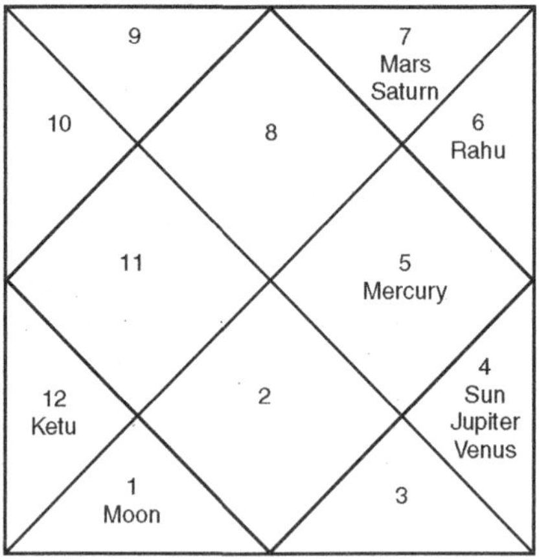

Sun = 118°24', Moon = 1°57', Mars = 197°16', Mercury = 125°19', Jupiter =102°33', Venus = 99°41', Saturn =203°6', Rahu = 178°13', Ketu = 358°13', Lagna = 230°7'.

Sun in the 9th house

Moon in the 6th house

Mars in the 12th house

Mercury in the 10th house

Jupiter in the 9th house

Venus in the 9th house

Saturn in the 12th house

Rahu in the 11th house

Ketu in the 5th house

A Few Observations:-

Moon's longitude of 1°57' means the native's birth took place in the asterism of Ashwini and the native's rasi is Mesha. The native was running the mahadasa of Ketu at the time of birth *(More on this in the next chapter)*.

The longitudinal difference of ~243° between the Moon and the Sun means that the tithi happens to be Krishna Paksha Shashti. Given that this falls under the 1st half of the tithi, the karana would be Garija.

The longitudinal sum of the Moon and the Sun is ~120° which happens to be Ganda yoga.

From our chapter on Lagna we can conclude that time of birth of 2:30 PM roughly translates into the rising sign moving into the 5th house from the sun sign as a result of which the Sun is placed in the 9th house in the birth chart.

The planets of Jupiter and Saturn are exalted in the native's rasi chart. The planet of Mercury is combust in this birth chart.

The planets of Saturn and Mars are conjunct while the planets of Sun, Jupiter and Venus are also conjunct.

Moon aspects both Mars as well as Saturn while both Saturn and Mars aspect the Moon. In addition to this Saturn aspects Jupiter, Sun and Venus while Jupiter aspects Ketu.

The native's lagna is Vrischika which is owned by Mars. This is likely to give the native a ruddy complexion and a fiery disposition which are characteristics of Mars. The native will be action oriented. Of course Vrischika being a water sign means the native would also be emotional and could be sensual being attracted to the fine arts and drama. Jupiter's aspect (Jupiter is in the 9th house) on the lagna is very auspicious indicating a certain amount of fortuitousness in life.

The 10th house which indicates the native's profession is Simha ruled by Sun. The native might be inclined towards and fare well in professions connected to the Sun such as politics, government, administration, law or a family business as the Sun also signifies the father figure. Mercury's presence in the 10th house of the birth chart indicates the native takes up a vocation which involves lots of analytical work such as business, trading, computers and technology or something related to communications. One possible interpretation of this is the native could be part of the government service with focus on information technology. The presence of Sun in the 9th house which owns the 10th house is an indicator of the native's potential interest in philosophy, religion and education. The native as a result could also be involved in the education sector be it in business or with the government.

The 2nd house which is an indicator of wealth here is Dhanus and ruled by Jupiter. Jupiter is also the natural significator of wealth and its placement in the 9th house in Kataka a sign where Jupiter is exalted indicates some amount of fortuity in the accumulation of wealth. Jupiter related professions such as finance and banking, law which can involve activities related to the sovereign might work for the native.

The 7th house which is an indicator of marriage and spouse here is Vrishaba and ruled by Venus which also happens to be the karaka for marriage. The 7th house is empty but Venus is placed in the 9th house which is the house of dharma, religion, higher education. The native may connect with the spouse through a school of learning or a religious gathering or in a foreign land. The spouse will have Venusian qualities which indicate interest in the fields of arts, music and drama.

The 5th house which signifies past life karma, creativity and entertainment as well as children sees the placement of Ketu in this house. Ketu is the planet of salvation and spirituality but being a malefic planet it adversely affects the native in the affairs of the 5th house. This native is however lucky as Jupiter which owns this house (Meena) is exalted and placed in the 9th house as a result of which it also aspects the 5th house which tends to negate the evil effects of Ketu. As we will see shortly in this chapter the planet of Ketu is vargottama meaning it occupies the same sign in both the rasi as well as the navamsa chart. This also nullifies to a great extent Ketu's placement in the 5th house.

Notice the conjunction of Sun, Jupiter and Venus which signify

Profession/Vocation, Marriage and Wealth in this birth chart. Saturn aspects all these planets and could delay the affairs of these planets.
The native's moon sign or rasi is Mesha which like the native's lagna Vrischika is ruled by Mars. Moon rules over the mind and the Mesha rasi native could be quick witted, full of novel ideas exhibiting a desire in the mind to take leadership or ownership of any task or situation. As Mesha rasi natives are known to rush into taking decisions the native must try and exhibit more practicality. Moon in this birth chart is afflicted by the aspect of both Mars and Saturn. The native must be very careful not to allow the mind to spiral out of control. Moon here is vargottama. This goes a long way in nullifying the negative effects of the 6th house where the Moon is placed which may include health issues, accidents, enemies as well as financial obligations. It can also nullify the negative effects of the lunar affairs which could mean anything related to your mother.

The native's Sun sign is Kataka or Cancer. Kataka is a water sign but also one of the cardinal signs. As the Sun sign reflects the native's personality, ego, temperament or anything that is exhibited to the outer world this native would possess the signs of a Cancerian which includes intensity as well as being emotional and sensitive to both the personal as well as the societal needs. The Kataka native exhibits passionate loyalty and is also a very good nurturer. This must however not be construed as being overbearing.

Bhava Chart:

We have thus far seen the principles and mechanics behind the construction of the rasi chart. The rasi chart divides the 360° zodiac into 12 equal parts so that each zodiac covers 30^0. We have, however seen that the rising sign times (refer rasimana and charakhandas in the chapter 12 Zodiacs or Rasis) for the 12 rasis vary even at the equator giving rise to the concept of long ascension and short ascension signs.This gives rise to the concept of a bhava chart where the longitudinal lengths of the 12 bhavas or houses vary unlike in a rasi chart which is simply divided into 12 30^0 zodiacs. The basis for the construction of the bhava chart lies in the formulation of the bhava madhyas (longitudinal cusps) especially the lagna and the madhya lagna. We have already seen methodology behind the calculation of the lagna. The madhya lagna is the middle point of the

10th house or midheaven. Recall in our chapter on the lagnas as well as in this chapter that the Sun is at its zenith in the sky at mean noon and it is likely to be placed in the 10th house of a birth chart at this point of time. This is considered by many to be the most important house in a birth chart. Calculation of the madhya lagna is critical in the construction of the bhava chart.

The following methods can be used for obtaining the madhya lagna:-

Method 1: Vedic Methodology

1. Obtain the dinardha on the day of birth (This is, of course, computed in the algorithm for obtaining the sunrise time)
2. Compute the birth time ghatika from sunrise Birth Time Ghatika = Local Mean Time of Birth – Local Mean Time of Sunrise
3. Compute the Natha at birth
   Natha = Birth Time Ghatika – Dinardha
   (Birth between Midday and Sunset)
   Natha = Dinardha - Birth Time Ghatika
   (Birth between Sunrise and Midday)
   Natha = Dinardha + Interval between birth and sunrise
   (Birth between Midnight and Sunrise)
   Natha = Dinardha + Interval between sunset and birth
   (Birth between Sunset and Midnight)
4. Obtain the Nirayana and Sayana Longitudes at sunrise on the given day (Already stated in sunrise time algorithm)
5. Compute the remainder degrees (See step 5 in computation of Lagna in the chapter on Lagna)
6. Intermediate = Natha – ((Remainder Degrees/30°) * (Rasimana at equator for rising sign at sunrise))
7. Meridian Distance = Remainder Degrees + ((Intermediate * 30°)/ (Rasimana at equator for rising sign at sunrise))
8. Madhya Lagna = Sayana Longitude at Sunrise + Meridian Distance – Ayanamsa

The madhya lagna obtained above in the mid-point of the 10th house or the midheaven.

Method 2: Trigonometric Method

The trigonometric methodology uses the same set of formulas as we had seen in the chapter on Lagna.

1. R = arctan ((sin (H) * tan (L)) / (cos ((sidereal time*15°) + H)))
2. Sayana Longitude of Cusp = arctan ((cos (R) * tan ((sidereal time*15°) + H))/ (cos (R + E)))
3. Nirayana Longitude of Cusp (Including Lagna) = Sayana Longitude of Bhava Madhya - Ayanamsa

H: Here H=0°; L: Latitude of the location; E: Obliquity of the ecliptic for the given year

Calculating Bhava Madhyas/ Bhava Sandhis

Now that we have the Lagna and the Madhya Lagna (Midheaven) we can calculate the mid-point (bhava madhyas) and end-points (bhava sandhis) of the 12 houses.

Lagna = Mid-point of 1st house (Udaya Lagna)

Mid-Point of 7th house = 180° + Lagna (Descendant or Asta Lagna)

Madhya Lagna = Mid-point of 10th house (Midheaven)
Mid-point of 4th house = 180° + Madhya Lagna (Patala)

Now that we have the mid-points of the 1st, 4th, 7th and 10th houses we can easily obtain the mid-points of the remaining 8 houses.

We simply trisect the arc between the 1st and 4th, 4th and 7th, 7th and 10th, and 10th and 1st house mid-points.

End-Point of any house = Mid-Point of preceding and succeeding houses.

For example, End-Point of 3rd House = (Mid-Point of 3rd House + Mid-Point of 4th House) / 2

The end point of any house is the starting point of the next house.

Example 8:

Compute the bhava chart for an individual born on **Friday, August 15, 2014 @ 2:30PM (14:30), New Delhi, India.**

We have computed the lagna as 230°7' or 20°7' Scorpio or Vrischika.

This becomes the mid-point of the 1st house.

Mid-Point of the 1st house = 230°7'

Mid-Point of the 7th house = 180° + Lagna = 50°7'

Let us now use the trigonometric method to calculate the midheaven.

R = arctan ((sin (H) * tan (L)) / (cos ((sidereal time*15°) + H)))

H=0°, thus the entire expression collapses to zero.

As a result, we obtain the following:-

Sayana Longitude of Cusp = arctan ((cos (0) * tan ((11h43m35s*15°) + 0))/ (cos (0 + 23.44)))

(Please refer appendix II and III for further information on E value and sidereal time)

Solving the above we get

Sayana Longitude of Cusp = 175.52°

Nirayana Longitude or Midheaven = 175.52° - 24.06° = 151°27' or 1°27' Virgo or Kanya.

Mid-Point of the 10th house = 151°27'

Mid-Point of the 4th house = 180° + Midheaven = 331°27'

Mid-Point of the 1st house = 230°7'

Mid-Point of the 7th house = 50°7'

Now let us calculate the mid-point of the remaining 8 houses:-

We compute the difference between two of the above 4 houses and trisect the number to obtain mid-point of remaining houses

(Mid-Point of the 10th house - Mid-Point of the 7th house) / 3 = 101°20'/ 3 = 33°47'

Mid-Point of 8th house = 33°47' + 50°7' = 83°54'

Mid-Point of 9th house = 33°47' + 83°54'= 117°41'

In a similar manner we obtain the mid-point of the other houses

(Mid-Point of the 4thhouse - Mid-Point of the 1st house) / 3 = 101°20' / 3 = 33°47'

Mid-Point of 2nd house = 33°47' +230°7' = 263°54'

Mid-Point of 3rd house = 33°47' + 263°54'= 297°41'

In a similar manner we obtain the mid-point of the other houses

Mid-Point of the 5th house = 357°41'

Mid-Point of the 6th house = 23°54'

Mid-Point of the 11th house = 177°41'

Mid-Point of the 12th house = 203°54'

Now that we have computed the mid-points (bhava madhya) for all the houses, we shall proceed to compute the end-points (bhava sandhi) of the 12 houses.

End-Point of 1st house = (Mid-Point of the 1st house + Mid-Point of 2nd house) / 2 = 247°

End-Point of 2nd house = (Mid-Point of the 2nd house + Mid-Point of 3rd house) / 2 = 280°47'

End-Point of 3rd house = 314°34'

End-Point of 4th house = 344°34'

End-Point of 5th house = 10°47'

End-Point of 6th house = 37°

End-Point of 7th house = 67°

End-Point of 8th house = 100°47'

End-Point of 9th house =134°34'

End-Point of 10th house = 164°34'

End-Point of 11th house = 190°47'

End-Point of 12th house = 217°

The Bhava Chart Table is as follows:

House	Starting Point	Mid Point	End Point	Planets Placed Here
1	217°	230°7'	247°	
2	247°	263°54'	280°47'	
3	280°47'	297°41'	314°34'	
4	314°34'	331°27'	344°34'	
5	344°34'	357°41'	10°47'	Moon, Ketu

6	10°47'	23°54'	37°	
7	37°	50°7'	67°	
8	67°	83°54'	100°47'	**Venus**
9	100°47'	117°41'	134°34'	**Sun, Mercury, Jupiter**
10	134°34'	151°27'	164°34'	
11	164°34'	177°41'	190°47'	**Rahu**
12	190°47'	203°54'	217°	**Mars, Saturn**

Interpreting the Bhava Chart:

The bhava sandhis or end-points of any of the above 12 houses also marks the starting point of the following house. For instance the end point of the 12th house is 217°. This also marks the starting point of the 1st house. Note how the longitudinal length of each of the 12 houses is not equal unlike in the rasi chart where each house is of length 30°.

Bhava Chart is considered critical in the vedic astrology community. As a result of the change in the longitudes of the 12 houses certain planets will be posited in the adjacent house in bhava chart vis-à-vis the rasi chart. In the above example, 3 planets would have their positions changed in the bhava chart when compared to the rasi chart. Moon is placed in the 5th house in the bhava chart (6th in rasi chart), Mercury in the 9th house (10th in rasi chart) and Venus in the 8th house (9th in rasi chart).

Many astrologers, when evaluating a horoscope, take the position of planets in a zodiac sign based on the rasi chart but will consider the house that the planet is posited in, based on the bhava chart. In the above example, Venus is placed in Kataka but as per the bhava chart is placed in the 8th house. Many consider the rasi chart when studying the general effects but use the bhava chart while evaluating specific results such as longevity and results of a dasa or bhukti. Planetary conjunctions and aspects are studied based on the rasi chart.

Divisional Charts / Navamsa:

We have often heard the term navamsa when approaching an astrologer for clarifications about our horoscope. Practitioners of vedic astrology lay great emphasis on navamsa when providing forecasts for an individual, especially when it is related to marriage. Navamsa is one of the divisional birth charts of vedic astrology. Navamsa is one among 16 important divisional charts or vargas that ancient texts have mentioned. Varga refers to the division of a zodiacal sign into parts. We have already studied the 27 nakshatras, each consisting of 4 padas earlier in this book. There are a total of 108 padas each with a longitude of 3°20'. These 108 padas are known to give rise to 108 potential divisional charts or vargas. The Brihat Parāśara Horāśāstra which is considered to be the most comprehensive extant work on vedic astrology defines 16 divisional charts or vargas on vedic astrology.

Rasi/Birth Chart -> D-1 -> General Matters -> 30° (longitude length per sign)

Hora Chart -> D-2 -> Wealth and Family -> 1°

Drekkana Chart -> D-3 -> Siblings -> 10°

Chaturthamsa Chart -> D-4 ->Fortune and Property -> 7°30'

Saptamsa Chart -> D-7 -> Children -> 4°17'8.5"

Navamsa Chart -> D-9 -> Spouse and Marriage ->3°20'

Dasamsa Chart -> D-10 -> Profession ->3°

Dwadasamsa Chart -> D-12 -> Parents ->2°30'

Shodasamsa Chart -> D-16 -> Vehicle and Comforts ->1°52'30"

Vimsamsa Chart -> D-20 -> Spiritualism ->1°30'

Chaturvimsamsa Chart -> D-24 -> Education and Knowledge ->1°15'

Saptavimsamsa Chart -> D-27 -> Strengths and Weakness ->1°6'40"

Trimsamsa Chart -> D-30 ->Evils and Bad Luck ->1°

Khavedamsa Chart -> D-40 -> Maternal Family, Auspicious and Inauspicious Events ->0°45'

Akshavedamsa Chart -> D-45 -> Paternal Ancestry, Fortune ->0°40'

Shastamsa Chart -> D-60 -> Past Life and Karma ->0°30'

Of the above sixteen we have already studied the rasi/birth/natal chart. The navamsa is the other divisional chart which is placed at a high premium when compared to the other vargas. Apart from studying the spouse and married/sex life, it is also studied to evaluate the strengths, weaknesses and the effects of the planets with respect to all areas of life. If a planet is badly placed in terms of its zodiac placement or positional placement (Position in a particular house) in the lagna chart but improves its position in the navamsa, then the negative effects of that planet are greatly reduced or even nullified and vice versa.

The intuition for the navamsa being the prince among the vargas follows from its longitudinal division of 3°20' or 1/9th division which is the span of 1 pada of a nakshatra. 9 padas constitutes a rasi or zodiac.

Vargottama: A planet that is occupying the same sign or rasi in both the rasi as well as the navamsa chart is said to be vargottama. It is derived from 2 words "Varga" meaning division and "Uttama" meaning best. As can be seen from its meaning a vargottama planet enhances its positive effects when it is already a benefic and greatly reduces or nullifies the negative effects when it is a malefic. An example would be Saturn's placement in Mesha where it is debilitated. If Saturn is placed in Mesha in both the rasi and navamsa chart then it is likely to reduce many evil effects and may confer many positive results to the native. A planet in vargottama is said to be more powerful than a planet in its exaltation sign.

The divisional charts assist the practitioners of vedic astrology in analyzing the horoscope of an individual to a great extent. For example, 2 individuals born on the same day could have all 9 planets placed in the same zodiac sign respectively. If they are born within short space of time of 2 hours, even their lagnas could be the same. A classic example of this are twins who are born within minutes of each other. This would mean their rasi charts (D-1) will also be the same. However, their destinies could be totally different. The marked difference in the divisional charts will aid an astrologer in providing accurate forecasts.

Mechanics of a Navamsa Chart: In example 7 of this chapter we have casted the rasi chart of an individual born at 2:30PM on Aug 15, 2014. The rasi chart of 2nd individual born on the same day at 2:00PM or even 3:00PM would be exactly the same. Why then would an astrologer provide different forecasts for the 2 individuals? This is where a divisional chart like the Navamsa comes into play. Navamsa is simply 1/9th division of a zodiac sign.This means that based on the longitude of the lagna and the

9 planets, 2 individuals born on the same day at 2:30PM and 3:00PM could have the same rasi chart but an entirely different navamsa chart.

The methodology of casting a navamsa chart is as follows:-

1. Calculate the nakshatra and nakshatra pada, based on the longitude of the lagna and the nine planets in the rasi chart
2. Based on the group classification place the nine planets and the lagna under one of the zodiacs, as per the tables below

Table 16: Nakshatra Navamsa Grouping

Group	Nakshatras
1	Ashwini, Rohini, Punarvasu, Magha, Hasta, Vishaka, Moola, Shravana, Purva Bhadrapada
2	Bharani, Mrigashirsha, Pushya, Purva Phalguni, Chitra, Anuradha, Purva Ashdha, Dhanishta, Uttara Bhadrapada
3	Krittika, Ardra, Ashlesha, Uttara Phalguni, Swati, Jyeshtha, Uttara Ashadha, Satabishak, Revati

Nakshatra Group	Pada – 1	Pada – 2	Pada – 3	Pada - 4
1	Mesha	Vrishaba	Mithuna	Kataka
2	Simha	Kanya	Tula	Vrischika
3	Dhanus	Makara	Kumbha	Meena

Example 9:

Compute the navamsa chart for an individual born on **Friday, August 15, 2014 @ 2:30PM (14:30), New Delhi, India.**

From example 7 and using the principles of table 16 and table 6 from the chapter on nakshatras, we can map the longitudes of the planets onto their respective nakshatra and padas.

Sun = 118°24' = Ashalesha Pada 4 = Meena

Moon = 1°57' = Ashwini Pada 1 = Mesha

Mars = 197°16’ = Swati Pada 4 = Meena

Mercury = 125°19' = Magha Pada 2 = Vrishaba

Jupiter = 102°33' = Pushya Pada 3 = Tula

Venus = 99°41'= Pushya Pada 2 = Kanya

Saturn = 203°6' = Vishaka Pada 1 = Mesha

Rahu = 178°13' = Chitra Pada 2 = Kanya

Ketu = 358°13' =Revati Pada 4 = Meena

Lagna = 230°7' = Jyestha Pada 2 = Makara

Navamsa Chart:

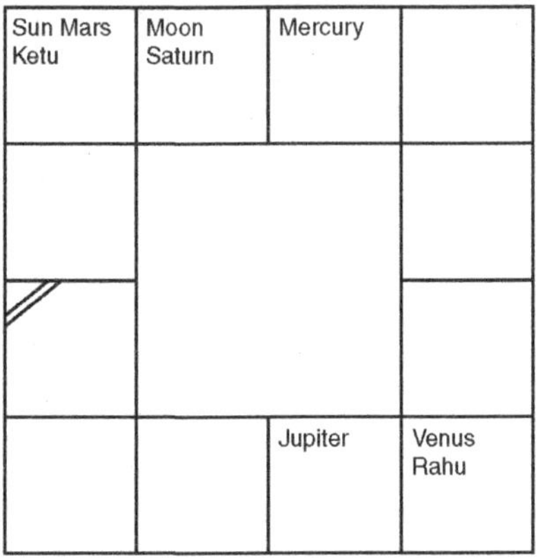

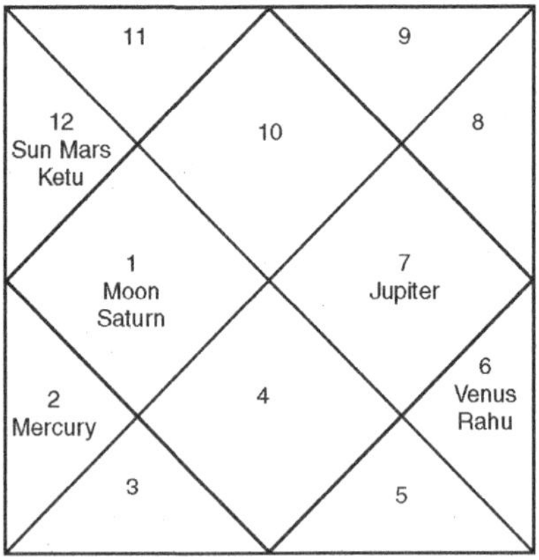

15

Dasa+ Bhukti / Main-Period + Sub-Period

The term “Dasa” or "Dasha" or “Mahadasa” in vedic astrology is used to indicate the main planetary period which an individual is under the influence of at a particular point in time. The planetary periods indicate when the good or bad effects are produced according to their placement by sign (Rasi), house (Bhava), combinations (Yogas or Raja Yogas) or aspects (Drishti). The Dasa Paddhati (system) of Directional Astrology is unique to vedic astrology; it is found in no other form of astrology. It symbolizes the overall direction of a person’s life for very long periods of time. There are many kinds of Dasa systems. Some are termed “Ayur Dasas” as they are used to only predict lifespan of an individual while others are “Phalita Dasas” as they can be used for all general purposes of life. Some are nakshatra based while some others are rasi based. Nakshatra based dasa system finds more traction as it is one of the limbs of the Panchang. Maharishi Parashara mentions 42 dasa systems out of which two are said to be used most frequently namely, "Vimshottari" and "Ashtottari".It is also mentioned that ashtottari dasa system is a conditional dasa system applicable only in select birth charts (It can be used for daytime births in Krishna paksha and nighttime births in Shukla Paksha) as a result of which the vimshottari dasa system which is applicable for all birth charts is the dasa system in vogue today. Vimshottari Dasa system is a Nakshatra Dasa System as it is derived from the Moon Sign Nakshatra. Some people also use the Nakshatra of the Lagna to make their forecasts but this is very uncommon given that the Lagna is calculated based on Sunrise and other factors while the Moon is the graha nearest to the Earth and has the maximum possible relative influence over Earth’s beings. For all practical purposes modern day astrologers follow the Moon sign nakshatra only.

Each dasa is controlled by one of the nine planets or navagrahas, and the quality and relative results of effects of each period is determined by the condition and position of that planet in the natal chart.

Vimshottari Dasa assumes that the maximum duration of life of an individual human being is 120 years which is the aggregate duration of all nine planetary periods as given below.

Table 17: Dasa Periods

Dasa	Period (Years)
Ketu	7
Venus	20
Sun	6
Moon	10
Mars	7
Rahu	18
Jupiter	16
Saturn	19
Mercury	17

As a result, the mahadasa of ketu lasts for 7 years for any individual while Jupiter mahadasa will long last for 16 years.The order of the main periods (dasa) under the Vimshottari dasa system is the dasa of Ketu followed by Venus, Sun, Moon, Mars, Rahu, Jupiter, Saturn, and Mercury. The first or initial mahadasa, however, varies for each individual based on the position and longitude of the Moon in the birth chart.

Calculation of Dasa Bhukti Periods

We have mentioned, many a time, in the book that the moon sign rasi is given a pre-eminent position in Vedic astrology much more so than the Sun Sign. One of the several reasons for this is the fact that the concept of dasa and bhukti is mainly based on the moon sign of an individual.

As mentioned in the previous para, the first mahadasa for each individual will be different and is based on the moon sign rasi and longitude of the moon in the birth chart. More specifically, the first mahadasa is based on the birth nakshatra or asterism of the individual. In our chapter on the nakshatras we mentioned the planetary ruler or lords of the 27 nakshatras. The first mahadasa for any native will be the lord of that nakshatra. For instance, if a native is born under the nakshatra of Punarvasu, the first mahadasa the native faces is Jupiter or Guru followed by Saturn, Mercury and so on. Similarly, if a native is born under the asterism of Uttara Phalguni, the first mahadasa for this native would be Sun or Surya Mahadasa followed by Moon, Mars and so on.

Balance of First Vimshottari Dasa

The first mahadasa is also the only mahadasa which may not run the entire course of its duration as shown in table 18. The Jupiter mahadasa for the Punarvasu born native may last for 16 years but it could also last for as less as a few hours which will be immediately followed by Saturn Mahadasa. This is based on balance period of the nakshatra under which the native is born.

Let us say the native takes birth at 2 PM on a Wednesday and the nakshatra of Punarvasu runs from 8 AM Wednesday to 8 AM Thursday. Six hours have elapsed since the start of this nakshatra. In this case the remainder of Jupiter mahadasa will be (24-6)/24 * 16 or 12 years which will be the number of years of the Jupiter mahadasa in the case of this native. This will, of course be, followed by 19 years of Saturn Mahadasa, 17 years of Mercury Mahadasa.

Bhukti

Each Mahadasa is subdivided into planetary periods called Antaradasa or Bhukti. Each antaradasa is further divided into Antarams which run their course in the same order as the mahadasa and with the same proportional duration.

The order of the bhuktis is the same as that of the mahadasa's with the first bhukti of a mahadasa being the same planetary sub-period. For example, the first bhukti of Mahadasa Ketu is Ketu/Ketu, the second is Ketu/Venus, the third Ketu/Sun and so on. These subdivisions allow a greater scope for detailed examination of the influence exerted by each mahadasa, and a much clearer indication of what events are expected to occur and when.

The Dasa-Bhukti of Jupiter-Venus will last for 16 years * Proportion of Venus' Period in vimshottari dasa system (20/120) = 16 * 20/120 = 2 Years 8 Months

The Dasa-Bhukti of Sun-Rahu will last for 6 * 18/120 = 10 Months 24 Days

The effect of various mahadasa's is highlighted as follows:-

Ketu Mahadasa

Ketu is a malefic planet but is also known as the planet of spirituality. The shadow planet Ketu is one of the most feared planets in astrology and is perceived to bring about the worst period in a native's life, as it is the carrier of hurdles and obstacles in life. The presence of impediments all around would make the native weaker from inside and would reduce his/her mental strength, peace and happiness. This period of ketu mahadasa would necessitate a lot of effort and hard work from the native though most of the efforts won't give worthy results due to Ketu's malefic influence. Since it is known as the planet of spirituality a native's thought under ketu mahadasa could turn towards god, religion, philosophy, renunciation and salvation (moksha). This can happen either if the native attains enormous amounts of wealth so that he/she is completely satisfied or if the effects of this dasa are disastrous which could lead the native to lose interest in life. The native could undertake several long religious journeys during this mahadasa.

The person undergoing ketu mahadasa could become insincere and reckless in this period and would confront many conflicts & quarrels which could lead towards differences and distances in professional and personal relations. The negative impacts of Ketu mahadasa could include fear from thieves, poison, fire and water, increasing foes, obstacles in education, accidents, unworthy travelling and losses in ventures. Ketu reaches maturity at the age of 48.

Venus Mahadasa

Venus is considered to be among the most benefic planets and is known as the planet of beauty, love,wealth and luxuries, and creativity and entertainment. Venus during its mahadasa could confer the native with enormous amounts of wealth, luxury and comfort and popularity. The native could shine in the fields of music, arts, cinema and theatre, media, business ventures including retail and luxury businesses such as jewellery industry. In addition to the above a well placed Venus could also confer the native with success in the financial services industry. A well placed Venus or Shukra would keep distress away and would bring all round prosperity, while hurdles won't leave much impact upon the native. The period of Venus or Shukra is also considered to be the most auspicious time for forming new relationships including marriage in the native's life. The native under Shukra Dasa would receive true respect and admiration from the surroundings in variant forms including some state honours. The native under the influence of shukra mahadasa would carry purity and trueness in core and thoughts and would get inclined towards pious and social pursuits. There would be remarkable growth in professional and financial stature while an ill-placed Venus in the birth chart could also bring some negative impacts including conflicts, distances and bitterness in relations, loss in ventures, financial constraints, opposition and restlessness. Venus reaches maturity at the age of 25.

Sun Mahadasa:

The planet of Sun is considered to be of royal bearing and is known to be the king among the 9 planet sand is thus considered to be positive and powerful and believed to bring potency and brilliance in the native's life. It can bestow upon the native with dominance and a very exalted position in society. Sun or Surya is believed to be a celestial body which brings luminous to the world and is also perceived to bring goodness in lives but as it signifies heat and aggression, the native could also be affected by these qualities. The natives under the influence of the Sun mahadasa are perceived to attain a strong position in the social circle, as they would receive the support of higher authorities, government institutes and the person would acquire power & authority but this period could also cause distance or separation from some close relations. In this period, people are perceived to receive good affluence from variant sources with significant involvement of pursuits related to medicines, weapons, fire, land and royalty. This is also the period when the native could succeed in any central themes such as government and politics and obtain a very high and prestigious position with fame and popularity. The Sun's ability to burn and extinguish any entity that comes near it also can cause the native to become anxious and restless and lack mental peace on account of the popularity and fame. This period also holds the fear and threat from thieves, enemies, government and fire along with some health problems including venereal diseases and fever. It could enclose the person and his closed ones with fears, distress and sorrow. Sun reaches maturity at the age of 22.

Moon Mahadasa:

Moon or Chandra is perceived to be a royal planet with immense purity and trueness and blesses one with divinity and wisdom. Moon is believed to be an explicit expression of beauty, charm and fantasy. Moon as we have already seen is known to rule the mind. An individual with a strong moon placement would have a strong and stable mind. The period of Moon could also lead the native to enter and excel in the fields of arts and entertainment as the planet Moon is also connected with luxury and comforts in a manner similar to Venus. It would be a period of beauty and splendor. Being a watery planet it also aids in success in water related professions which can include agricultural, gardening and farming related activities. Moon is the explorer of spiritual portraits, as it leads the person towards spiritualism and makes him/her walk the divine path. This period could be marked by intellectual growth and the native could attain acknowledgement and exalted positions with increased social and financial standing which would bring in happiness and immense satisfaction to the person. As Moon is soft and feminine in nature, it could also bring about popularity with females. A weak and adverse placement of Moon or Chandra in the birth chart could bring mental weakness and laziness and could make the native indulge in quarrels and conflicts which could also make an individual repel good pursuits leading to gradual decrease in wealth. Moon reaches maturity at the age of 24.

Mars Mahadasa:

Mars or mangal is a warrior planet and is considered to be the most aggressive planet among the navagarahas. Its fierce and fiery nature makes it a malefic planet although it is known to do several positive things. It expresses authority and power and provides the same to the natives which results in persistence and patience. In general, planet Mars or mangal enhances the possibilities of foes and is known to induce the feeling of enmity in the mind of the native. Mangal would also make the person stand firm and potent. It may defend the person from any harm if posited favourably and could make the native triumphant. Mars during its dasa can confer upon the native with success in martial and military pursuits as well as success in fields such as sports and security related themes. It could also confer the native with positions of authority, especially in government and politics. The adverse placement of planet Mars or mangal could bring about negative impacts in this period as the person could have danger from fire and thieves and may lose some of his/her wealth, besides imprisonment could also be possible. Distances and differences could arise in relations while health issues, possibilities of accident, body aches, urinary problems, kidney problems and pain in eyes are possible. On the whole, it would be a period of activity and movement but there could be much anxiety and lack of peace. Mars reaches maturity at the age of 28.

Rahu Mahadasa:

Rahu is one of the two illusionary planets of vedic astrology and is among the most malefic planets perceived to bring adverse impacts on human life. It makes the life of a person tough and brings about harshness and hurdles in the native's life. It is known to be the planet of materialistic desires and gambling tendencies. The natives under the influence of the shadow planet Rahu would be made to confront many obstacles. It could make the native very unstable with fluctuations in life which brings about distress to the native. The native could see many failures and could face loss of wealth as well in this phase. The native could get involved in immoral and evil deeds in this period and would get inclined towards materialistic pleasures and indulge in acts such as gambling, besides which there would be fears due to thieves, poisonous stuff, weapons and authority. The native could make many enemies and could face separation from his/her closed ones. There could be some diseases including veneral diseases, asthma, urinary ailments and weakness are possible. Rahu is known to confer very sudden results which can catch the native off-guard whether the result is positive or negative. Rahu if positively placed can confer upon the native with spectacular results even to the extent of obtaining kingly status from being a pedestrian overnight. Rahu reaches maturity at the age of 42.

Jupiter Mahadasa:

The planet Jupiter or Guru is the best benefic in vedic astrology as it is known to bring about many positives in a native's life, during its mahadasa period. Jupiter is the giver of true wisdom and knowledge as leads us down the path of prosperity and happiness bestowing upon the native with many positives including status, marriage, children, land and buildings. As its name suggests, it is the best teacher. It is the planet of dharma and acts as a friend, philosopher and guide. Jupiter or Guru in its mahadasa makes the person see the right things in the right direction and take the right decisions which in the right perspective could aid the native towards astronomical professional heights and could endow him/her with great financial strength as well. People would emerge wiser in this period or and will attain reverence from the surroundings which will lead them towards a strong and dominant position. The person under Jupiters or brihaspati's mahadasa would receive positive impact upon mind and would have pure thoughts and perceptions which would take him/her over the righteous path, besides which he/she would be inclined towards spiritual and religious aspects of life. He/she would stay close to pious people and go about sacred pursuits. In this period, the native would acquire true knowledge and would emerge wiser. Happiness and bliss could be attained more easily by any native during the Jupiter mahadasa. The native under Jupiter mahadasa could excel in fields such as law, banking and finance, education, advisory roles such as a minister to a king. As Jupiter is known to expand everything, a person under the influence of Jupiter mahadasa could also experience weight gain. Jupiter reaches maturity at the age of 16.

Saturn Mahadasa:

Quite simply the planet of karma, Saturn or Shani is perceived to be one of the most powerful and dominant planets in vedic astrology holding a unique position among the 9 planets. While it is believed to bring about negative impacts on the native when posited unfavourably in the birth chart, Saturn or Shani in its Mahadasa could bring in name, fame and success reaching dizzy heights when it is a benefic. It is also the planet of longevity. Saturn is the supreme purifier, as it makes the person walk through difficult times and leading them towards success.

Saturn's mahadasa bestows upon the person with immense potency and domination in personality as in the period of Saturn, the native would stand strong and effective; besides, he/she would triumph over obstacles and would walk towards heights of fame and respect and attain high authority. In the Saturn mahadasa, the native would be endowed with the strength of intellect and knowledge; in addition he/she would get truly inclined towards pious and social pursuits; and in the end, the native would emerge as a modest and wiser personality through a tough process. The native could engage in more public interaction and enter the political arena. Saturn mahadasa would be a period of many fluctuations and instability, but it would bring peace and satisfaction towards the end; and the person would appear as having gone through a cleansing process. The Saturn mahadasa could enclose the person with increasing enemies who would try to harm the native at their best while the native would become more aggressive and irksome in the Saturn's Mahadasa. Distances and conflicts in relations around could be another adverse impact of Saturn dasa; besides, ill-placement of Saturn could also lead towards imprisonment and opposition with the authorities. Saturn when unfavourably placed could destroy the native causing destruction of wealth, conflicts and all-round misery. In the end, Saturn impacts are always the blend of both good and bad but it always takes the person towards the positive direction in the end. Saturn reaches maturity at the age of 36.

Mercury Mahadasa:

The planet Mercury or Budha known to be the prince among the navagrahas is a supremely positive planet, as it takes the person towards the heights of intellect and wisdom and bringing about brilliance in profession and personality. Mercury or Budha brings about optimism in the person along with trueness and purity in thoughts and takes the native along a righteous and ethical path. As this planet rules education, communication, commerce and trade, the native will tend to excel in academic pursuits during this period and could also attain professional success as a negotiator, communicator, marketing or sales agent. Mercury is also known to aid the native in achieving success in the financial services industry, in particular in stock trading and broking as well as excelling in trade related businesses. It will almost be a period of blessings as the person would find admirable growth in the professional and financial stature; quite apart from this, there would be a positive growth in relations around the native. The native in Budha mahadasa would get inclined towards creative aspects of life, for which the person could get involved in art, music, drama and poetry. The person would turn more towards intellectual and philosophical pursuits and would learn a lot in this period. The person in the Budha Mahadasa period would attain excellence and precision in this period through his/her sincerity, determination and dedication. Mercury reaches maturity at the age of 32.

The above effects of the mahadasas are only generic observations and vary from individual to individual. In reality the entire duration of a mahadasa rarely does only good or bad and the results are mixed in nature. Within each mahadasa the results of the various bhuktis would also depend on planetary positions in the birth chart.

In judging the effects of dasas and bhuktis the following factors need to be taken into account

1. Placement of the Mahadasa (and Bhukti) planet in different zodiacs or rasis (Exaltation Sign, Debilitation Sign, Own Sign, Friend's Sign, Enemy's Sign, Neutral Sign)
2. Placement of the Mahadasa (and Bhukti) planet in different houses in a birth chart
3. Position of the Mahadasa (and Bhukti) planet relative to the Moon in the birth chart
4. Any potential conjunctions or aspects with/other planets of the mahadasa planet in the birth chart
5. Whether the mahadasa planet is a functional benefic or malefic of the Lagna
6. Position and zodiac sign of the mahadasa planet in the divisional charts such as navamsa (Rasi Chart is, of course, of utmost importance).

In the next chapter, we will discuss the concept of planetary transits including the famed sade sati. Practitioners of vedic astrology in general place more importance to the effects of a mahadasa over and above that of the effects of a planetary transit. It has been said that the results of a very favourable mahadasa will nullify the effects of a weak planetary transit. Similarly, if an individual is under the influence of an unfavourable mahadasa even an excellent planetary transit might not be of any help.

16

Gochara Transit

The word Gochara can be divided into 2 parts 'Go' meaning Globe and 'Chara' meaning movement. It simply means movement of globes. Gochara is simply transits of the planets from the position of Moon in a birth chart (Our Moon Sign Rasi). It is the transit technique used by professional astrologers today. Some classical texts also state that transit of planets must conditionally be looked at from the position of the Lagna till the age of 33 post which the Moon centric Gochara system can be used.

The transiting planet is affected by its position from the Moon. Its general indications and the things ruled by its lordship of houses are favourably or unfavourably affected by the planet's position from the Moon. The Moon, as we mentioned earlier represents growth and one's mind. If the planet is favourably affected by its position from the Moon, then it can grow its significations. If the planet is in an unfavourable position, then the opposite is true.

We have already mentioned the time taken for the 9 planets to traverse a rasi. The Sun, Venus and Mercury on an average take 30 days to traverse a zodiac, while Mars takes about 45 days to 2 months on average. Moon takes 2.25 days, Jupiter 1 year, Rahu & Ketu 1.5 years and Saturn 2.5 years.

The planetary transits of Jupiter, Saturn, Rahu and Ketu are assigned the most importance given the longer duration taken by these planets in completing a revolution with Jupiter and Saturn transits placed at a premium given that Rahu and Ketu are illusionary in nature (Mathematical Nodes). We often hear the terms Guru Peyarchi and Shani Peyarchi with regards to the Jupiter and Saturn Transit. These are the 2 largest planets of our Solar System and their slow moving nature, especially that of Saturn which is a karmic or practical planet coupled with the best benefic and the worst malefic nature respectively means their transits will produce long term effects.

Saturn's transit from the Moon is the most important transit event because Saturn is the one planet that gives long term effects and puts into motion those events of life that will have the strongest karmic effects. Sade Sati is a much feared time in a person's life. This is when Saturn transits the 12th, 1st, and 2nd sign from the native's Moon Sign or Rasi. A Kanya Rasi native faces the Sade Sati period when Saturn transits Simha, Kanya and Tula Rasis. Each Saturn transit last for approximately 2.5 years and the 3 signs together total 7.5 years; hence the term sade sati.

During this time, Saturn cannot create long term effects. Saturn creates life changing, long term effects like marriage or major career changes when transiting beneficial houses from the natal Moon. When transiting unfavourable houses from the Moon, Saturn cannot give strong, long term implications.

Sun:

The Sun conveys status, authority and power to the person. It will also give vitality and robust health. When the Sun transits favourably from the natal Moon, one can expect these significations, to grow. In unfavourable positions, expect the opposite.

The Sun is favourable if transiting the 3rd, 6th, 10th and 11th (Upachayas) from natal Moon.

The Sun is unfavourable when transiting the 1st, 2nd, 4th, 5th, 7th, 8th,9th and 12th house from natal Moon.

Moon:

The Moon represents our mind, its growth and its stable nature, comfort and our attitude. When the Moon transits favourable positions from its natal placement, then everything in general runs more smoothly and there is a sense of comfort and happiness. When the Moon transits bad placements from its natal position, then there is more stress and a lack of tranquility.

The transiting Moon is favourable when it is transiting the 1st, 3rd, 6th, 7th, 10th and 11th from the natal Moon. The transiting Moon is unfavourable when it is transiting the 2nd, 4th, 5th, 8th, 9th and 12th from the natal Moon.

Mars:

Mars represents will power, the ability to fight and win battles, the energy to overcome obstacles, physical ability and courage, our siblings, and our experiences with our house and any real estate or land (Mars or Bhauma reared by bhumi devi) we may own. When Mars is transiting favorable houses, we will be able to utilize the energy of Mars constructively and benefit on the above significations.When Mars is transiting unfavourable houses from the Moon, then there will be more stress related to the above issues.

Mars is favourable when it transits the 3rd, 6th and 11th house from the natal Moon.

Mars is unfavourable when it transits the 1st, 2nd, 4th, 5th, 7th, 8th, 9th, 10th, and 12th house from natal Moon.

Mercury:

Mercury represents communications like speech, reading, writing, technology etc. It also signifies trade and commerce. Mercury signifies one's friends, business, social contact and ability to manifest desires concretely. It is the planet that signifies analytical ability in a native. One can expect these significations to grow when Mercury is transiting good houses from the natal Moon while there will be problems with these things when Mercury transits bad houses from Natal Moon.

Mercury is favourable when it transits the 2nd, 4th, 6th, 8th, 10th and 11th house from the natal Moon. Mercury is unfavourable when it transits the 1st, 3rd, 5th, 7th, 9th and 12th house from the natal Moon.

Jupiter:

Jupiter is the planet of dharma, religion, philosophy and righteousness, and represents one's aspirations and the ability to live up to those aspirations. Jupiter will show whether someone follows their inspirational path and do what they are meant to do in life. This means they could use wisdom and sound reasoning to solve the most pressing issues. Jupiter represents the teachers and mentors in our life. When Jupiter transits favourable houses, we will have good experiences with our teachers and they will be able to guide us beneficially. When Jupiter transits unfavourable houses, our dharma and our life do not line up. There are obstacles and setbacks to achieving the destiny we imagine for ourselves. Jupiter is not able to grow that destiny. Jupiter is favourable transiting the 2nd, 5th, 7th, 9th, and 11th house from the natal Moon.

Jupiter is unfavourable transiting the 1st, 3rd, 4th, 6th, 8th, 10th and 12th house from the natal Moon.

Venus:

Venus represents materialistic desires and being able to see the worth in things. It is recognizing the inherent value in everything that comes into our lives. Venus will show us the path of not paying too much for something of little value and the path to avoiding devaluing those things which are precious. The Moolatrikona sign of Venus is Libra, the Scales. The Scales will weigh what is more valuable and give the person the ability to make the correct decision. Venus rules negotiation and sharing. When Venus transits bad houses from the Moon, our sense of value becomes slightly skewed and our ability to see the value of things diminishes. When transiting good houses from the natal Moon, Venus will show us the correct decision and the inherent value of our experiences.

Venus is favorable when transiting the 1st, 2nd, 3rd, 4th, 5th, 8th, 9th, 11th, and 12th houses from the natal Moon.

Venus is unfavorable when transiting the 6th, 7th and 10th houses from the natal Moon.

Saturn:

Saturn is the number one planet of destiny. Saturn rules time, longevity and karma, thus it rules long term effects in a person's life like major career events, marriage, childbirth, buying a new home, etc. When Saturn is transiting a good house from the Moon, it is able to grow long term effects that will be with the native a very long portion of their lives. When Saturn is transiting a bad house from the Moon, Saturn's ability to grow these long term, life changing effects is diminished. When Saturn transits the 12th, 1st, and 2nd houses from the Moon, it is unable to grow these long term significations. This is known as the sade sati period which is feared by many in the vedic astrology community. Transiting Saturn is favourable in the 3rd, 6th and 11th houses from the Moon.

Transiting Saturn is unfavourable in the 1st, 2nd, 4th, 5th, 7th, 8th,9th,10th, and 12th houses from the Moon.

Example 10: 7.5 year Saturn period for a simha rasi native.

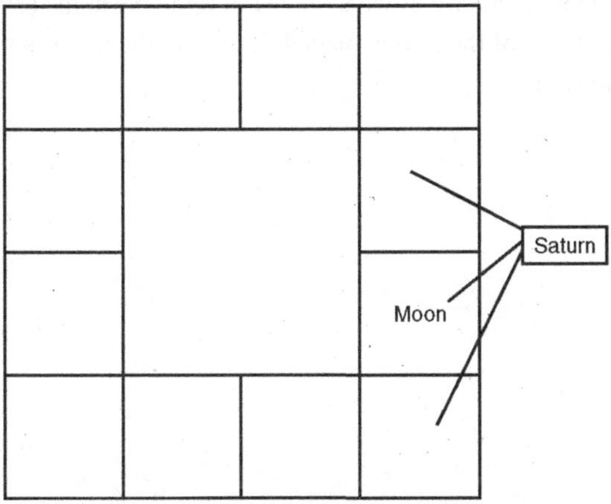

For a native born in Simha rasi when Saturn transits through Kataka, Simha and Kanya rasis the native is undergoing a sade sati phase of his/her life. As Saturn takes 2.5 years to transit through one rasi it will take 2.5 * 3 or 7.5 years to transit through 3 signs. Saturn being a karmic planet has an effect on our long term karma. Being an elderly and slow moving planet it tends slow down any action we plan to undertake in our lives. This is enhanced during the sade sati period. As such it is a period when our patience and resolve is tested and necessitates additional effort in all our undertakings. It is not necessarily a bad period as is thought by many. It could be thought of as a period of examination which during our schooldays some of us excelled at. As Saturn takes 30 years to complete one full revolution, every individual will face 1 round of sade sati by the time he/she is 30 years of age.

Rahu and Ketu:

Rahu and Ketu are north and south lunar nodes of Moon. As such their behaviour sare determined by the zodiac sign and the owner of the zodiac sign they are placed in. Their behaviour is also governed by the planets they are conjunct with or aspected by.

Transiting Rahu and Ketu are favorable in the 3rd, 6th and 11th houses from the Moon.

Transiting Rahu and Ketu are unfavorable in the 1st, 2nd, 4th, 5th, 7th, 8th,9th,10th, and 12th houses from the Moon.

Given Rahu and Ketu are always placed in opposite signs (7th from each other) even if one of the two is placed favorably the other is placed in an unfavorable sign.

Appendix 1

Rasimana + Charakhanda

We have already studied the concepts of rasimana and charakhanda. Rasimana is simply the rising periods of the 12 zodiacs at the equator.We have also seen that the inclination of the plane of the ecliptic implies that the rising periodsa vary for the 12 rasis. Additionally we must note that rasimana numbers will always be tropical or sayana as the world follows solar standard times and not sidereal times.

Table 1: Rasimana of Rasis at Equator

Group	Rasis				Rasimana (Asus*)	Rasimana (Hours)
I	Aries	Virgo	Libra	Pisces	1674	1h51m36s
II	Taurus	Leo	Scorpio	Aquarius	1795	1h59m40s
III	Gemini	Cancer	Sagittarius	Capricorn	1931	2h08m44s

Note: 1 Asu = 4 Seconds.

We have also seen that the term charakhanda or ascensional difference is used to refer to the variation in rising periods of the 12 rasis at different latitudes (ascensional variation).

Indian astronomers used several devices in ancient times to ascertain the time of the day. Among the instruments that were used was a hindu sundial and Gnonom also known as a shanku where the shadow of a vertical rod is applied on a horizontal plane in order to ascertain among other data the latitude of the location. With the help of such a hindu dial one could on the day of the equinox measure the length of the mid-day shadow of a shanku of 12 units length for any latitude. The length of this mid-day equinotical shadow for any latitude multiplied by 10, 8 and 3.333 would enable us to obtain the charakhanda values (in vighatis)for the 3 groups of signs in the above table respectively.

Table 2: Length of mid-day equinotical shadow and charkhanda values in vighatis and asus

Latitude	Length	Vighati 1	Vighati 2	Vighati 3	Asu 1	Asu 2	Asu 3
1°	0.21	2.1	1.68	0.70	12.6	10.08	4.2
2°	0.42	4.2	3.36	1.40	25.2	20.16	8.4
3°	0.63	6.3	5.04	2.10	37.8	30.24	12.6
4°	0.84	8.4	6.72	2.80	50.4	40.32	16.8
5°	1.05	10.5	8.4	3.50	63	50.4	21
6°	1.26	12.6	10.08	4.20	75.6	60.48	25.2
7°	1.47	14.7	11.76	4.90	88.2	70.56	29.4
8°	1.69	16.9	13.52	5.63	101.4	81.12	33.8
9°	1.9	19	15.2	6.33	114	91.2	38
10°	2.11	21.1	16.88	7.03	126.6	101.28	42.2
11°	2.33	23.3	18.64	7.77	139.8	111.84	46.6
12°	2.55	25.5	20.4	8.50	153	122.4	51
13°	2.7	27	21.6	9.00	162	129.6	54
14°	2.99	29.9	23.92	9.97	179.4	143.52	59.8
15°	3.21	32.1	25.68	10.70	192.6	154.08	64.2
16°	3.44	34.4	27.52	11.47	206.4	165.12	68.8
17°	3.66	36.6	29.28	12.20	219.6	175.68	73.2
18°	3.9	39	31.2	13.00	234	187.2	78
19°	4.13	41.3	33.04	13.77	247.8	198.24	82.6
20°	4.37	43.7	34.96	14.57	262.2	209.76	87.4
21°	4.6	46	36.8	15.33	276	220.8	92
22°	4.85	48.5	38.8	16.17	291	232.8	97
23°	5.09	50.9	40.72	16.97	305.4	244.32	101.8
24°	5.34	53.4	42.72	17.80	320.4	256.32	106.8
25°	5.59	55.9	44.72	18.63	335.4	268.32	111.8
26°	5.85	58.5	46.8	19.50	351	280.8	117
27°	6.11	61.1	48.88	20.37	366.6	293.28	122.2
28°	6.38	63.8	51.04	21.27	382.8	306.24	127.6
29°	6.65	66.5	53.2	22.17	399	319.2	133

30°	6.93	69.3	55.44	23.10	415.8	332.64	138.6
31°	7.21	72.1	57.68	24.03	432.6	346.08	144.2
32°	7.5	75	60	25.00	450	360	150
33°	7.79	77.9	62.32	25.97	467.4	373.92	155.8
34°	8.09	80.9	64.72	26.97	485.4	388.32	161.8
35°	8.4	84	67.2	28.00	504	403.2	168
36°	8.71	87.1	69.68	29.03	522.6	418.08	174.2
37°	9.04	90.4	72.32	30.13	542.4	433.92	180.8
38°	9.37	93.7	74.96	31.23	562.2	449.76	187.4
39°	9.72	97.2	77.76	32.40	583.2	466.56	194.4
40°	10.06	100.6	80.48	33.53	603.6	482.88	201.2
41°	10.43	104.3	83.44	34.77	625.8	500.64	208.6
42°	10.8	108	86.4	36.00	648	518.4	216
43°	11.19	111.9	89.52	37.30	671.4	537.12	223.8
44°	11.58	115.8	92.64	38.60	694.8	555.84	231.6
45°	12	120	96	40.00	720	576	240
46°	12.42	124.2	99.36	41.40	745.2	596.16	248.4
47°	12.87	128.7	102.96	42.90	772.2	617.76	257.4
48°	13.33	133.3	106.64	44.43	799.8	639.84	266.6
49°	13.8	138	110.4	46.00	828	662.4	276
50°	14.3	143	114.4	47.67	858	686.4	286
51°	14.82	148.2	118.56	49.40	889.2	711.36	296.4
52°	15.35	153.5	122.8	51.17	921	736.8	307
53°	15.92	159.2	127.36	53.07	955.2	764.16	318.4
54°	16.52	165.2	132.16	55.07	991.2	792.96	330.4
55°	17.13	171.3	137.04	57.10	1027.8	822.24	342.6
56°	17.79	177.9	142.32	59.30	1067.4	853.92	355.8
57°	18.46	184.6	147.68	61.53	1107.6	886.08	369.2
58°	19.2	192	153.6	64.00	1152	921.6	384
59°	19.97	199.7	159.76	66.57	1198.2	958.56	399.4
60°	20.78	207.8	166.24	69.27	1246.8	997.44	415.6

2

Equation of Time

We have already seen that the equation of time is a concept that tracks the difference between two conventions of the motion of the sun one that tracks the movement of the sun and another which describes the motion of the sun setting 2 successive noons 24 hours apart. Before the invention of modern clocks equation of time was used to set clocks. It is essentially the difference between the civil time and solar time.

Equation of Time = Mean Time – Apparent Time at any moment (whichever is greater).

For the mathematically and astronomically inclined the equation of time is equal to the sum of two sine curves and can be approximately calculated using the following formula:-

EoT (Equation of Time) = (9.87 * sin (2D) - 7.53 * cos (D) - 1.5 * sin (D)) * (-1)

where

D =360 * (N-1) / 365 (N is the day number of the year)

Example 1:

Calculate the equation of time for August 15, 2014

August 15th is the 227th day of the year 2014.

D = 360 * (227-81)/365 = 144

EoT = (9.87 * sin (2*144) - 7.53 * cos (144) - 1.5 * sin (144)) * (-1) = ~4 minutes

Thus the Equation of Time for August 15th, 2014 is +4 minutes.

The two sine curves in reality reflect two astronomical effects namely the earth's axial tilt and its orbital eccentricity that cause the equation of time to vary on a day to day basis. The equation of time value is zero when a planet's axial tilt and orbital eccentricity are both zero.

The earth's axial tilt also known as the obliquity of the ecliptic is the angle between its rotational axis and its orbit. Its value is currently said to be 23.44 degrees. The earth's precession of the equinoxes or just precession is said to be caused due to the change in the orientation of its rotational axis.

Obliquity of the Ecliptic could be obtained using the following formula:-

$\varepsilon = 23° 26' 21.45'' - 46.815'' T - 0.0006'' T^2 + 0.00181'' T^3$(T is the number of Julian centuries since 2000)

Example 2:

Calculate the obliquity of the ecliptic for August 15, 2014

The T value here is 5340 days since the start of the century divided by the number of days in a century (36525 days) or T = 0.146

Substituting this value in the above formula we get $\varepsilon = 23.44°$

The second astronomical effect that causes the variation in the equation of time is of course earth's orbit around the sun which is elliptical with variable speed and not orbital with constant speed which causes the sun to appear to move faster with respect to the fixed stars. The eccentricity of earth's orbit is about 0.0167.

Table 3: Equation of Time Values

Date	Jan	Feb	Mar	Apr	May	Jun	Jul	Aug	Sep	Oct	Nov	Dec
1	4	14	13	4	-3	-2	3	6	0	-11	-16	-10
2	4	14	13	4	-3	-2	4	6	-1	-11	-16	-10
3	5	14	13	4	-3	-2	4	6	-1	-12	-16	-9
4	5	14	12	3	-3	-2	4	6	-1	-12	-16	-9
5	5	14	12	3	-3	-2	4	6	-2	-12	-16	-9
6	6	14	12	3	-3	-2	4	6	-2	-13	-16	-8

7	6	14	12	2	-4	-1	5	5	-3	-13	-16	-8
8	7	14	12	2	-4	-1	5	5	-3	-13	-16	-7
9	7	15	11	2	-4	-1	5	5	-3	-13	-16	-7
10	7	15	11	2	-4	-1	5	5	-4	-14	-16	-6
11	8	15	11	1	-4	-1	5	5	-4	-14	-16	-6
12	8	15	10	1	-4	0	5	5	-4	-14	-15	-6
13	9	15	10	1	-4	0	5	5	-5	-14	-15	-5
14	9	15	10	1	-4	0	5	4	-5	-15	-15	-5
15	9	15	10	0	-4	0	6	4	-5	-15	-15	-4
16	10	15	9	0	-4	0	6	4	-6	-15	-15	-4
17	10	14	9	0	-4	1	6	4	-6	-15	-14	-3
18	10	14	9	-1	-4	1	6	4	-7	-15	-14	-3
19	11	14	8	-1	-4	1	6	3	-7	-16	-14	-2
20	11	14	8	-1	-4	1	6	3	-7	-16	-14	-2
21	11	14	8	-1	-4	1	6	3	-8	-16	-13	-1
22	12	14	8	-1	-3	2	6	3	-8	-16	-13	-1
23	12	14	7	-2	-3	2	6	2	-8	-16	-13	0
24	12	14	7	-2	-3	2	6	2	-9	-16	-13	0
25	12	14	7	-2	-3	2	6	2	-9	-16	-12	0
26	13	14	6	-2	-3	2	6	1	-9	-16	-12	1
27	13	13	6	-2	-3	3	6	1	-10	-16	-12	1
28	13	13	6	-2	-3	3	6	1	-10	-16	-11	2
29	13	3	5	-3	-3	3	6	0	-11	-16	-11	2
30	13	13	5	-3	-3	3	6	0	-11	-16	-11	3
31	14	13	5	-3	-2	3	6	0	-11	-16	-10	3

3

Sidereal Time

We have already seen that the sidereal time is a time-keeping system used by astronomers to keep track of the direction to point their telescopes to view a given star in the night sky. It is a time scale that is based on the Earth's rate of rotation measured relative to the fixed stars. Just as how we use clocks to tell time or how in ancient times people used the sundial to tell time and locate the position of the sun in the sky, astronomers from a given observation point use telescopes and other instruments to locate the position of a particular star in the sky. If a star is found at a particular point in the sky on one night at a specified sidereal time then it will be found again at the same sidereal time the following day. As mentioned earlier the calculations of the longitudes of all planets are based on sidereal times. Given that the human race is accustomed to civil and solar times based on the position of the sun with respect to the earth we always compute longitudes, sunrise and lagna by first calculating the tropical or sayana longitudes and then use the ayanamsa to obtain their nirayana or sidereal equivalents.

There are two types of sidereal times (In a similar manner to a solar time) namely local apparent sidereal time (LAST) and local mean sidereal time (LMST). Local apparent sidereal time is the hour angle of the vernal equinox at a particular location. The LMST differs from LAST by not more than 1-2 seconds as a result of nutation or wobbling motion of the earth's axis of rotation.

The following formulae(implementable in Microsoft Excel) could be used in obtaining the local mean and apparent sidereal times:-

Days (Julian Days) =367*year-INT(7*(year+INT((month+9) 12))/4)+INT(275*month/9)+day-730531.5 + (hours + minutes/60 + seconds/3600)/24

T (Julian Centuries) = Days / 36525

LMST = MOD(280.46061837 + 360.98564736629 * Days, 360) + Longitude of Location

(Year, Month, Day, Hours, Minutes and Seconds is the Universal Date and Time or GMT or 0° longitude, MOD function is used to calculate the remainder. INT function calculates the integer value of a number)

D1 (Mean Longitude of Ascending Node)= MOD(125.04452 - 1934.136261 * T, 360)

D2 (Mean Longitude of Sun) = 280.461 + 0.9856474 *Days

D3 (Mean Longitude of Moon)=MOD(218.3164591+481267.88134236 *T-0.0013268*T^2+T^3/538841-T^4/65194000,360)

DP (Change in ecliptic longitude due to nutation) = -17.2*SIN(D1) -1.32*SIN(2*D2) -0.23*SIN(2*D3) +0.21*SIN(2*D1)

DE (Angle Shift) = 9.2*COS(D1) +0.57*COS(2*D2) + 0.1*COS(2*D3) -0.09 *COS(2*D1)

EPS (Obliquity of Ecliptic) =$23° 26' 21.45'' - 46.815'' T - 0.0006'' T^2 + 0.00181'' T^3$

Difference = DP*COS(DE+EPS)/3600 (This is the difference between mean sidereal time and apparent sidereal time)

LAST = Difference + LMST

Example 3:

Calculate the sidereal time on **Friday, August 15, 2014 @ 2:30PM (14:30), New Delhi, India.**

The time of 14:30 hrs is 2:30 PM IST which equates to GMT of 9 hours (9:00 AM)

Applying the above date and time and using a longitude of 77.2° we get similar values for LMST and LAST of 11 hours 43 minutes and 35 seconds.

4

Longitude of Sun and Moon

While using the trigonometric approach to calculating the sidereal time we have also looked we have come across a set of intermediate formulas D1, D2 and D3. These are the mean longitudes of ascending node of the moon, the sun and the moon respectively.Mean longitude is the longitude of a planet if its orbit were circular, free of any gravitational pulls with zero inclination. We of course know that the orbit of Earth around the Sun is elliptical with an axial tilt. The ecliptic longitude of a planet is obtained when we adjust for orbital eccentricities, orbital inclinations and nutations. This concept is applicable for the Moon and Sun as well.

Sun:

The longitude of Sun can be calculated using the following formula:-

L = 280.461 + 0.9856474 *Days (Number of Julian Days since Jan 1,2000)

G = 357.528 + 0.9856003 * Days

Sayana Longitude of Sun = L + 1.915 * sin(G) + 0.020 * sin(2*G)

Nirayana Longitude of Sun = Sayana Longitude of Sun – Ayanamsa

When calculating the longitude of the Sun one must be aware of the fact that it is the Earth that orbits around the Sun as a result of which the position and time for calculating any astronomical data is relative between these two astronomical bodies.

Example 4:

Calculate the longitude of Sun at **Friday, August 15, 2014 @ 2:30PM (14:30), New Delhi, India.**

Applying a D of 5,340 days we obtain a sayana longitude of 142.47°. Deducting the ayanāmsa (24.06°) we obtain the nirayana longitude of the Sun which is 118°24'.

Moon:

The Moon's orbit around the Earth is elliptical and its mean inclination to the ecliptic plane is about 5°.

The Moon's orbit around the Earth is strongly perturbed by the gravitational pull of the Sun and is subject to a number of anamolies including evection, variation and annual inequality all of which alter the velocity of the motion of the Moon. As a result its ecliptic longitude is calculated using the following set of formulas.

Mean Longitude of Moon =MOD(218.3164591+481267.88134236*T-0.0013268*T^2+T^3/538841-T^4/65194000,360)

D = MOD(297.8502042+445267.1115168*T-0.00163*T^2+T^3/545868-T^4/113065000,360)

M = MOD(357.5291092+35999.0502909*T-0.0001536*T^2+T^3/24490000,360)

M' = MOD(134.9634114+477198.8676313*T+0.008997*T^2+T^3/69699-T^4/14712000,360)

F = MOD(93.2720993+483202.0175273*T-0.0034029*T^2+T^3/3526000-T^4/863310000,360)

A1 =MOD(119.75+131.849*T,360)

A2 =MOD(53.09+479264.29*T,360)

A3 = MOD(313.45+481266.484*T,360)

Additives = 3958*SIN(A1) + 1962*SIN(D3-F) + 318*SIN(A2)

Longitude Vectors (Sum of 60 terms):-

L1 = 6288774*SIN(0*D +0*M+1*M' +0*F)
L2 = 1274027*SIN(2*D +0*M-1*M' +0*F)
L3 =658314*SIN(2*D +0*M+0*M' +0*F)
L4 =213618*SIN(0*D +0*M+2*M' +0*F)

L5 =185116*SIN(0*D +1*M+0*M' +0*F)
L6 =114332*SIN(0*D +0*M+0*M' +2*F)
L7 =58793*SIN(2*D +0*M-2*M' +0*F)
L8 =57066*SIN(2*D -1*M-1*M' +0*F)
L9 =53322*SIN(2*D +0*M+1*M' +0*F)
L10 =45758*SIN(2*D -1*M+0*M' +0*F)
L11 =40923*SIN(0*D +1*M-1*M' +0*F)
L12 =34720*SIN(1*D +0*M+0*M' +0*F)
L13 =30383*SIN(0*D +1*M+1*M' +0*F)
L14 =15327*SIN(2*D +0*M+0*M' -2*F)
L15 =12528*SIN(0*D +0*M+1*M' +2*F)
L16 =10980*SIN(0*D +0*M+1*M' -2*F)
L17 =10675*SIN(4*D +0*M-1*M' +0*F)
L18 =10034*SIN(0*D +0*M+3*M' +0*F)
L19 =8548*SIN(4*D +0*M-2*M' +0*F)
L20 =7888*SIN(2*D +1*M-1*M' +0*F)
L21 =6766*SIN(2*D +1*M+0*M' +0*F)
L22 =5163*SIN(1*D +0*M-1*M' +0*F)
L23 =4987*SIN(1*D +1*M+0*M' +0*F)
L24 =4036*SIN(2*D -1*M+1*M' +0*F)
L25 =3994*SIN(2*D +0*M+2*M' +0*F)
L26 =3861*SIN(4*D +0*M+0*M' +0*F)
L27 =3665*SIN(2*D +0*M-3*M' +0*F)
L28 =2689*SIN(0*D +1*M-2*M' +0*F)
L29 = 2602*SIN(2*D +0*M-1*M' +2*F)
L30 =2390*SIN(2*D -1*M-2*M' +0*F)
L31 =2348*SIN(1*D +0*M+1*M' +0*F)
L32 =2236*SIN(2*D -2*M+0*M' +0*F)
L33 =2120*SIN(0*D +1*M+2*M' +0*F)
L34 =2069*SIN(0*D +2*M+0*M' +0*F)
L35 =2048*SIN(2*D -2*M-1*M' +0*F)
L36 =1773*SIN(2*D +0*M+1*M' -2*F)
L37 =1595*SIN(2*D +0*M+0*M' +2*F)
L38 =1215*SIN(4*D -1*M-1*M' +0*F)
L39 =1110*SIN(0*D +0*M+2*M' +2*F)
L40 =892*SIN(3*D +0*M-1*M' +0*F)
L41 =810*SIN(2*D +1*M+1*M' +0*F)

L42 =759*SIN(4*D -1*M-2*M' +0*F)
L43 =713*SIN(0*D +2*M-1*M' +0*F)
L44 =700*SIN(2*D +2*M-1*M' +0*F)
L45 =691*SIN(2*D +1*M-2*M' +0*F)
L46 =596*SIN(2*D -1*M+0*M' -2*F)
L47 =549*SIN(4*D +0*M+1*M' +0*F)
L48 =537*SIN(0*D +0*M+4*M' +0*F)
L49 =520*SIN(4*D -1*M+0*M' +0*F)
L50 =487*SIN(1*D +0*M-2*M' +0*F)
L51 =399*SIN(2*D +1*M+0*M' -2*F)
L52 =381*SIN(0*D +0*M+2*M' -2*F)
L53 =351*SIN(1*D +1*M+1*M' +0*F)
L54 =340*SIN(3*D +0*M-2*M' +0*F)
L55 =330*SIN(4*D +0*M-3*M' +0*F)
L56 =327*SIN(2*D -1*M+2*M' +0*F)
L57 =323*SIN(0*D +2*M+1*M' +0*F)
L58 =299*SIN(1*D +1*M-1*M' +0*F)
L59 =294*SIN(2*D +0*M+3*M' +0*F)
L60 =0*SIN(2*D +0*M-1*M'-2*F) = 0

Longitude Vector Sum = Sum of L1 through L60
Sayana Longitude of Moon = Mean Longitude of Moon + ((Longitude Vector Sum + Additives)/1000000) + Change in ecliptic longitude due to nutation

Nirayana Longitude of Moon = Sayana Longitude of Moon - Ayanamsa

Example 5:

Calculate the longitude of Moon at **Friday, August 15, 2014 @ 2:30PM (14:30), New Delhi, India.**
Applying the above formulae we get:-
Mean Longitude of Moon = 18.626°
(Longitude Vector Sum + Additives)/1000000= 7.3861°
Sayana Longitude of Moon = 26.015°
Nirayana Longitude of Moon = 1°57'

5

Auspicious and Inauspicious Times

Abhijit Muhurtha

Abhijit Muhurat or Muhurtha is auspicious time during midday which approximately lasts for 48 minutes or 2 ghatikas. Abhijit Muhurat is capable of destroying innumerable doshas and it is considered one of the best Muhurats to start all sort of auspicious works. It also goes by the term of vijay muhurtha. According to one version in the puranas it is the 4th lagna from the lagna (clockwise or counter-clockwise). It is the time when the Sun is placed in the 10th house or the house of karma of a birth chart.

Abhijit Muhurat is the 8th Muhurat out of 15 Muhurats of duration 48 minutes or 2 ghatikas each (48 mins * 15 = 12 hours) which prevail between the sunrise and the sunset. The time interval between the sunrise and the sunset is divided into 15 equal parts and the middle portion of fifteen parts is known as Abhijit Muhurat.

If the sunrise occurs at 6 a.m. and the sunset occurs at 6 p.m. for a particular location then Abhijit Muhurat would start exactly 24 minutes before midday and would end after 24 minutes of midday. In other words Abhijit Muhurat for such a location would be between 11:36AM to 12:24PM of the day. Due to seasonal change of sunrise and sunset timings, the exact time and duration of Abhijit Muhurat is not fixed.

It is believed that Lord Shiva killed demon Tripurasur during Abhijit Muhurat.

The counter part of Abhijit Muhurat is Nishita Kaal which prevails during midnight.

It should be noted that Abhijit Muhurat is not suitable on Wednesday as it forms a malefic Muhurtha on this weekday.

Rahukaalam

The planet of Rahu is one of the malefic planets among the navagrahas. It is considered inauspicious and is known as a planet of the asuras. We have already seen the history behind Rahu and his planetary status. Rahu being an asura planet is more powerful at night but during the day it imposes ~1.5 hour or 90 minute period termed as Rahukaalam which is considered as very inauspicious for initiating any new venture or activity or undertaking a journey or buying /selling assets (transaction). Needless to say it is an inauspicious time for marriage or for that matter entering a new house.

To calculate Rahukaalam, the time between the sunrise and sunset is divided into 8 equal units or time-groups, with each time-group mapped onto a particular weekday to obtain the rahukaalam time. If the day happens to be of duration of 12 hours then rahukaalam would last for 12/8 or 1.5 hours during the day. For each weekday, Rahukaalam falls as under:-

- Sunday – 8th Unit
- Monday – 2nd Unit
- Tuesday – 7th Unit
- Wednesday - 5th Unit
- Thursday – 6th Unit
- Friday – 4th Unit
- Saturday – 3rd Unit

If we assume a 6 AM sunrise and a 6 PM sunset rahukaalam timings would look like this:-

Sunday: 4.30 p.m. - 6.00 p.m.
Monday: 7.30 a.m. - 9.00 a.m.
Tuesday: 3.00 p.m. - 4.30 p.m.
Wednesday: 12.00 p.m. - 1.30 p.m.
Thursday: 1.30 p.m. - 3.00 p.m.
Friday: 10.30 a.m. - 12.00 p.m.
Saturday: 9.00 a.m. - 10.30 a.m.

Gulika

Gulika which some people also term as Maandi is said to be the son of Saturn or Manda. It is a shadow planet just like Rahu and Ketu. Some people believe that that any activity carried out during Gulika(Flowering Time) period will be repeated once again as aresult of which some people start activities like building a house, buying assets or vehicles. Marriages of course should not be conducted.

There is an interesting legend behind the genesis of gulika. Ravana the 10-headed king had imprisoned all the 9 planets during his reign and had forced the 9 planets to be positioned at a very auspicious location for the birth of his son Indrajit so that he could become invincible. 8 planets obeyed him while the 9th planet Saturn which was posited in the 11th house managed to stretch its legs and place it in the 12th house. An infuriated Ravana chopped off Saturn's legs which managed to throw its flesh and blood onto the Lagna at the particular point of time which created 'Gulika'. Gulika is the symbol of our ego. Some people believe that an outstanding birth chart can be spoiled by influence of Gulika in much the same way as pride and ego are known to vitiate many good qualities in human beings. Gulika works better when placed in the 10th or 11th houses which are Saturn's natural ruling signs (makara and kumbha). It is not considered auspicious when posited in the lagna. Gulika is known to affect the affairs of the house it is posited in.Kalidasa's Uttara Kalamrita however states that Guilka and Maandi are not synonymous. They are said to be the 2 sons of Saturn.

For a day birth Maandi's position is at the end of the 26,22,18,14,10,6 and 2 ghatis after sunrise in the sequence of weekdays starting from Sunday. For Wednesday it will be after the end of 14 ghatis after sunrise. A day (sunrise to sunset) as we know conists of 30 ghatis.For a night birth Maandi's position is at the end of the 10,6,2,26,22,18 and 14 ghatis after sunset in the sequence of weekdays starting from Sunday. A night (sunset to sunrise) as we know consists of 30 ghatis.For a day birth Gulika's position is determined by dividing the duration of the day into 8 parts and counting from the lord of the weekday Gulika's position is at the end of Saturn's part. For a Sunday day birth Gulika would be the period just before sunset.For a night birth Gulika's position is determined by dividing the duration of the day into 8 parts and counting from the lord of the 5th day from the current weekday Gulika's position is at the end of Saturn's part. For a Sunday night birth we have to count from Thursday (5th day) and Saturn here will be the 3rd part of the night.

If we assume a 6 AM sunrise and a 6 PM sunset gulikatimings would look like this:-

Sunday: 3 p.m. - 4.30 p.m.
Monday: 1.30 p.m. - 3 p.m.
Tuesday: 12 p.m. - 1.30 p.m.
Wednesday: 10.30 a.m. - 12 p.m.
Thursday: 9 p.m. - 10.30 a.m.
Friday: 7.30 a.m. - 9 a.m.
Saturday: 6 a.m. - 7.30 a.m.

Yamagandam

This is also considered to be very inauspicious. Yamagandam means death time.Only death ceremonies are performed during Yamagandam. Any activity commenced during this time invites the 'death' of the work or energies relating to that work as a result of which activities during Yamagandam leads to a failure or destruction of the end-result. Yamagandam is known to be the son of Jupiter.

If we assume a 6 AM sunrise and a 6 PM sunset yamagandam timings would look like this:-

Sunday: 12.00 p.m. - 1.30 p.m.
Monday: 10.30 a.m. - 12.00 p.m.
Tuesday: 9 a.m. - 10.30 a.m.
Wednesday: 7.30 a.m. - 9 a.m.
Thursday: 6 a.m. - 7.30 a.m.
Friday: 3 p.m. - 4.30 p.m.
Saturday: 1.30 p.m. - 3 p.m.

6

Table of Navagrahas

Table 4: Planetary Sign Dignities

Planet	Own Sign(S)	Moola-trikona Sign	Exaltation Sign	Debilita-tion Sign	Approximate Time Spent in One Zodiac
Sun	Simha	Simha (0-20°)	10°Mesha	10° Tula	1 Month
Moon	Kataka	Vrishaba (2-20°)	3° Vrishaba	3° Vrischika	2.25 Days
Mars	Mesha + Vrischika	Mesha (0-12°)	28° Makara	28° Kataka	45-60 Days
Mercury	Mithuna + Kanya	Kanya (16-20°)	15° Kanya	15° Meena	1 Month
Jupiter	Dhanus + Meena	Dhanus (0-10°)	5° Kataka	5° Makara	1 Year
Venus	Vrishaba + Tula	Tula (0-15°)	27° Meena	27° Kanya	1 Month
Saturn	Makara + Kumbha	Kumbha (0-20°)	20° Tula	20° Mesha	2.5 Years
Rahu					1.5 Years
Ketu					1.5 Years

❑❑❑